HOW TO MAKE LEMONADE

A Spiritual Journey:
Transforming Your Life
One Lemon at a Time

Melanie Dees

HOW TO MAKE LEMONADE

A Spiritual Journey:
Transforming Your Life
One Lemon at a Time

ISBN 13: 978-0-9705008-9-2

Copyright © 2011 – Melanie Dees

www.jjpublishingonline.com

CONTENTS

CONTENTS

CONTENTS

CONTENTS

FOREWORD

God Bless You,

Reflect on each devotional as you read, and determine what it means to you. Ask God to impart in your heart the things that you need to change to develop a closer relationship with him. Salvation is not given as a group or family plan but an individual relationship plan between you and Christ. He is not asking you to change anything; neither is he asking you to be perfect. He is asking you to have a heart for him and to give your life to him totally and completely. God loves you beyond your comprehension. You have never had a man; woman, girlfriend or boyfriend who can love you with the intensity that Christ loves you and gave his life for you. They can love you with the love of Christ but not as Christ loves you. You will never be the same. As you read this devotional, reflect on each and every event in your life and elevate it in the spirit to determine the value of the lesson and ask yourself: Is this a lemon or lemonade? If it's a lemon make lemonade, if its lemonade sit back and enjoy the refreshments.

God Bless You for Planting a Seed in My Life

ACKNOWLEDGEMENTS

I thank my heavenly Father for trusting me
To do a work for Him.
I thank Him for the many Jewels
I have had an opportunity to meet and minister-to.
Many; others thought, were Tools to be used.
They are all Diamonds in His sight.

"Come and hear, all ye that fear God and I will declare unto
you what HE hath done for my soul."
Psalm: 66:16

DEDICATION

To my children
Kayla Patrice,
Tabitha DeMa'ria Faith
Chaste'y Yolanda
Tai Elizabeth
The Hardy's

To
My Natural Family
My Blood Washed Family
Tita Johnson
Apostle Bishop Sammy C. Smith
Grace Cathedral Ministries

To
Every Person that has entered my life
Thank you,
Special Thanks to
Linda Franklin
William C. Hairston

SPECIAL DEDICATION

To my Mother, Willie Mae, my Aunts Dorothy Bell and Margaret and my Uncle Richard

When you awoke this morning did you think of yourself as a Tool or a Jewel? An item of beauty or an item to be used for someone's personal gain, or did you see yourself as a thing of value to be admired and treasured by all? Aren't you glad man looks at the outside, but God Looks at the heart? What determines the quality of a gift, the package or the content?

A Time for Everything

There is a time for everything, and a season
for every activity under heaven:
a time to be born and a time to die, a time to plant
and a time to uproot,
a time to kill and a time to heal, a time to tear
down and a time to build,
a time to weep and a time to laugh, a time to mourn
and a time to dance,
a time to scatter stones and a time to gather them,
a time to embrace and a time to refrain,
a time to search and a time to give up, a time to keep and a time
to throw away, a time to tear and a time to mend,
a time to be silent and a time to speak,
a time to love and a time to hate, a time for war
and a time for peace.

What does the worker gain from his toil?
I have seen the burden God has laid on men.
He has made everything beautiful in its time. He has also set
eternity in the hearts of men; ye they cannot fathom what God
has done from beginning to end.

I know that there is nothing better for men than to be happy and
do good while they live.
That everyone may eat and drink, and find satisfaction in all his
toil—this is the gift of God.
I know that everything God does will endure forever; nothing
can be added to it and nothing taken from it. God does it so that
men will revere him.
Whatever is has already been, and what will be has been before;
and God will call the past to account.

And I saw something else under the sun: In the place of
judgment—wickedness was there, in the place of justice—
wickedness was there.
I thought in my heart, "God will bring to judgment both the
righteous and the wicked, for there will be a time for every
activity, a time for every deed."
I also thought, "As for men, God tests them so that they may see
that they are like the animals.
Man's fate is like that of the animals; the same fate awaits them
both: As one dies, so dies the other. All have the same breath;
man has no advantage over the animal. Everything is
meaningless.

All go to the same place; all come from dust, and to dust all return.

Who knows if the spirit of man rises upward and if the spirit of the animal goes down into the earth?" So I saw that there is nothing better for a man than to enjoy his work, because that is his lot. For who can bring him to see what will happen after him?

Ecclesiastes 3:1-22

BROKEN GLASS

This devotional is the result of brokenness. While sitting in the car one day, I noticed that there was broken glass all around me. To the untrained eye that is all that was there, but to a glassblower or someone who works with glass, that broken glass represented a new creation. A master craftsman can take the broken glass and melt it down and recast it to make something more beautiful. This is exactly what Christ does with us. When we become broken, He is able to recast us into an image of His dear Son.

Scripture: The sacrifices of God are a broken spirit; a broken and contrite heart, O God, you will not despise. **Psalms 51:17**

My Thoughts for Making Lemonade:

_____

_____

_____

_____

_____

TOOLS

What is a tool, except a device to get a particular job done? Primitive, modern or new age their result is to accomplish a task. A tool can be any hand-or machine-operated device employed, as with manually applied force or by means of motor power. The outcome is a means of achieving something else; making a task that may have been impossible, easy. Tools are items used in the course of everyday work.

In many cases when someone of seeming greater power wants to control another person they will often manipulate that individual. Somebody who is easily manipulated becomes the tool of someone's destruction, especially to carry out unpleasant or dishonest tasks that they may be unwilling to do.

Your imagination can be a tool of Satan to discourage and discredit you. His goal is to derail your purpose in God. He will bring back to your memory those things of pain or failure to discourage you from moving forward in God.

Satan sends negative comments through those we love. They become instruments of pain. The impressions or comments vary and become permanent. Words are like ammunition. They can protect or destroy. Thoughts become much like a bookbinder's implement. The imprint made in our mind is as though it's been made with the tool which is used to press a design into leather, cloth, or paper. The stamped design is permanently impressed on the object. Satan uses this method to define us as Christians and to try to discredit us as believers.

Each time we hear the negative comment, the impression becomes more indelible, and we begin to believe we're the imprint that has been made. Satan tells us how unworthy we are, that we're not good enough for God and that He can never use someone like us. He tells us how people view us and why we can't be used by God to encourage others to seek the Lord for deliverance.

Scripture: The thief comes only to steal and kill and destroy; Jesus said, I have come that they may have life, and have it to the full. **John 10:10**

Saints of the highest God must be sober, and vigilant; Cast all your anxiety on him because he cares for you. Be self-controlled and alert. Your enemy the devil prowls around like a roaring lion looking for someone to devour. Resist him, standing firm in the faith, because you know that your brothers throughout the world are undergoing the same kind of sufferings. **I Peter 5:7-9**

We must keep our mind stayed on God and trust in him. For though we live in the world, we do not wage war as the world does. The weapons we fight with are not the weapons of the world. On the contrary, they have divine power to demolish strongholds. We demolish arguments and every pretension that sets itself up against the knowledge of God, and we take captive every thought to make it obedient to Christ. And we will be ready to punish every act of disobedience, once our obedience is complete.
II Corinthians 10:3-6

My Thoughts for Making Lemonade:

_____

_____

_____

_____

_____

_____

_____

JEWELS

Jewels are gemstones or precious minerals that are treasured for their beauty and durability. Their value generally depends on four elements: the beauty of the stone itself; its clarity; its hardness and toughness; and the skill with which it has been cut and polished. Stones such as diamonds, rubies, and emeralds represent one of the greatest concentrations of money value. During times of war or economic disturbance, many people convert their wealth into precious stones, which are transportable and more easily sold.

The beauty of gems depends to a large extent on their visual properties. The most important visual properties are the degree of refraction and color. Other characteristics include fire, the display of colors; the ability to present two different colors when viewed in different directions, and transparency. Diamonds are highly prized because of their fire and brilliancy.

The appearance of a gem as seen by reflected light is another visual property of gemstones and is called luster. Luster is particularly important in the identification of gemstones in their uncut state. A gem cannot always be identified by sight alone. It is therefore necessary to rely on measurement of the optical properties that can be determined without harming the stone in any way.

Gems are shaped entirely by being grounded on abrasive wheels or revolving coarse disks. The first step in the cutting of a gem is to saw it roughly to shape. Thin abrasive disks or metal disks charged with powdered diamond or other abrasives are employed in this process.

As the people of God, we are often tried by fire. The trials and test of life that may seem so unfair at the time are to strengthen us and to bring us closer to Christ. So the surgery, the wreck, the missed promotion, the lost job, or broken relationships were all to bring out the shine in you, because you will come out as pure gold.

Scripture: See, I have refined you, though not as silver; I have tested you in the furnace of affliction. For my own sake, for my own sake, I do this. **Isaiah 48:10**

My Thoughts for Making Lemonade:

_____

_____

_____

_____

_____

WHAT IS A DIAMOND?

Diamonds reflect back the light reflected on them: they project it in several directions.

A diamond is a mineral form of carbon, valued as a precious stone, and used for various industrial purposes. Diamonds occur in various forms and is the hardest substance known. Diamonds form at great depths within the earth and are typically billions of years old.

Hardness varies in every diamond with the direction of the cut. Diamonds exhibit a wide range of transparency and color. Quality diamonds of clear, strong, and those with unusual colors are highly prized. The name "diamond" is derived from the Greek word adamas ("invincible"). Two important properties contribute to a diamond's beauty, brilliance and fire. Brilliance is the fraction of the light that falls on a diamond, which the diamond returns to the eye of an observer—the more light returned, the higher the brilliance.

The primary object of diamond cutting is to bring out the fire and brilliance. The tools used for cleaving are simple, but great skill is needed in their use because too hard a blow applied in the wrong direction may ruin the stone.

A diamond cutter seeks to enhance the brilliance and fire of each stone and to eliminate imperfections, such as cracks and cloudiness. The cutter develops a plan that will accomplish these goals while still producing a gem of the greatest size and hence maximum value.

A diamond in the rough is a diamond in its natural state, a person, or thing of fine quality but lacking polish.

Examining the stone is the first step in diamond cutting, which is much like recognizing the qualities in children. Children are like diamonds, in which they are hard and resistant to change based on the peer pressures and emotional pressures. It takes an experienced counselor or teacher to see beyond the display of character the youth may exhibit to produce the diamond expected.

The different facets of an individual's life must be considered. Every child will not become a marquis or a star diamond, but each child does have some qualities that can be developed. Many children spend the day caring for their siblings and mother; a mother who may be sick, addicted to drugs, overworked, or does not have a husband in the home.

Children with a negative attitude that needs to be addressed may not know how to express themselves; therefore our short vision only allows us to see someone who could do better not someone who is trying and needs encouragement. We must tell them they are important and someone finds them special.

The children of the Lord are the same; we each possess a quality that can be used in the Kingdom, but sometimes we just need someone to encourage us.

Scripture*:* Sons are a heritage from the Lord, children a reward from him. Like arrows in the hands of a warrior are sons born in one's youth. **Psalms 127:3-4**

Do not give any of your children to be sacrificed to Molech, for you must not profane the name of your God I am the Lord. **Leviticus 18:21**

My Thoughts for Making Lemonade:

_____

_____

_____

_____

_____

_____

_____

AGES AND STAGES OF SAINTHOOD
From a child to a man

God does not require us to be perfect but to be purposed. In our efforts to impress others, we're at times disappointed because we're not prepared to accept the criticism that may follow. Receiving Christ as our Lord and Savior offers a new birth into the body of Christ. He expects us to learn and grow, maturing from a babe to a teen in the spirit by accepting responsibility, praying and trusting. As we mature, the trials may intensify, but as a young adult in Christ we understand trials and test. Christ offers increased maturity and an opportunity for us to be an adult in the spirit praying others through some of their battles. Grow Up!

Scripture: When I was a child, I talked like a child; I thought like a child, I reasoned like a child. When I became a man, I put childish ways behind me. **I Corinthians 13:11**

My Thoughts for Making Lemonade:

_____

_____

SAD

SEX, ALCOHOL AND DRUGS

Sex is exciting for the minute and satisfies a desire for touch, but it cannot touch the most intimate part of your mind and body. Alcohol is numbing to the senses, but it cannot remove the pain of a thought, touch, or event. Drugs will change your outlook for a minute, but it cannot change the spirit, only the Spirit of God can do that. Yes, it is our body but all of the above substances have negative and long term consequences if used incorrectly. Our body is the temple of God, and we cannot introduce negative thoughts or actions into it without negative consequences.

Scripture: Therefore, I urge you, brothers, in view of God's mercy, to offer your bodies as living sacrifices, holy and pleasing to God—this is your spiritual act of worship. Do not conform any longer to the pattern of this world, but be transformed by the renewing of your mind. Then you will be able to test and approve what God's will is his good, pleasing and perfect will. **Romans 12:1**

 My Thoughts on Making Lemonade:

_____

_____

_____

_____

_____

_____

_____

_____

_____

_____

_____

_____

_____

_____

_____

_____

_____

_____

_____

_____

_____

_____

WHAT?

What does money buy? Can you take the money with you when you die? Can money buy happiness? Can money make you well? What if you die today? What if you failed in school or work? What if your parents die? What if your siblings die? What are you doing to have eternal life?

Scripture: What good will it be for a man if he gains the whole world, yet forfeits his soul? Or what can a man give in exchange for his soul? **Matthew 16:26**

My Thoughts for Making Lemonade:

_____

_____

_____

_____

_____

_____

_____

_____

_____

_____

MOTHER

Mother is the first person we see in the morning and the last person we see at night. The first voice we hear when we purpose to make a decision. The last voice we hear when we choose to disobey. Our thoughts are interrupted by our mother's voice in the worst situation. Our decisions and actions are governed by her voice. When we choose to go astray it's her voice we hear.

The voice of Christ is the same. It will give us instruction so that when we are in the situation we can make the best decision. Very much the same way our mother will not force us neither will the Holy Ghost.

Scripture: Train a child in the way he should go, and when he is old, he will not turn from it. **Proverbs 22:6**

My Thoughts on Making Lemonade:

_____

_____

_____

_____

_____

YOU!

Consider this; you are the guarantor of your destiny. You are your greatest hero! You are your greatest critic and whether you realize it or not, you can also be your greatest enemy. You can be your hindrance. You can also be the reason for your failures. You are the reason for your success. When you listen to your soul and not your spirit, you become the violator of your future. What did the Lord say about *you*?

Scripture: I know that nothing good lives in me, that is, in my sinful nature. For I have the desire to do what is good, but I cannot carry it out. For what I do is not the good I want to do; no, the evil I do not want to do—this I keep on doing. Now, if I do what I do not want to do, it is No longer I who do it, but it is sin living in me that does it. So I find this law at work: When I want to do good, evil is right there with me. For in my inner being, I delight in God's law; but I see another law at work in the members of my body, waging war against the law of my mind and making me a prisoner of the law of sin at work within my members. What a wretched man I am! Who will rescue me from this body of death? Thanks be to God—through Jesus Christ our Lord! So then, I myself in my mind am a slave to God's law, but in the sinful nature a slave to the law of sin. **Romans 7:18-25**

My Thoughts on Making Lemonade:

_____

_____

_____

_____

_____

_____

_____

_____

_____

_____

_____

_____

_____

_____

_____

_____

_____

_____

_____

FLY

Several days ago I was sitting in my office when I noticed a common housefly, buzzing around the office. He would land, and I would attempt to swat him but to no avail. Eventually, he landed near enough for me to make a quick swat and whack, he was dead, or so I thought. Before I could place him in a trash receptacle, he had revived himself and flew away. Sin is very much the same way. It is very elusive initially, but it begins to get closer and closer. We think we have killed the desire to sin until it rears its head again. Until we are dead to sin, it will continue to provoke us.

Scripture: Therefore do not let sin reign in your mortal body so that you obey its evil desires. Do not offer the parts of your body to sin, as instruments of wickedness, but rather offer yourselves to God, as those who have been brought from death to life; and offer the parts of your body to him as instruments of righteousness. For sin shall not be your master, because you are not under law, but under grace. **Romans 6:12-14.**

My Thoughts on Making Lemonade:

_____

_____

_____

_____

_____

_____

_____

_____

_____

_____

_____

_____

_____

_____

_____

_____

_____

_____

_____

_____

_____

GOLD

Gold is a highly sought-after precious metal used for jewelry, arts, coins and medicine. It is dense, soft, shiny and the purest metal known. It has served as a symbol of wealth throughout history. Gold is insoluble in nitric acid, which dissolves other metals. This is where we get the term failed the "acid test" because nitric acid is used to determine if gold is in certain items. Throughout our lives we will be tested and only those that are pure gold will come forth. Gold is tested by fire. As the fire gets hotter, the gold achieves its purest form. Therefore, each time we have a test we get closer to God because our endurance level increases, which creates a more perfect and pure person. We cannot be defeated!

Scripture: See, I have refined you, though not as silver; I have tested you in the furnace of affliction. For my own sake, for my own sake, I do this. How can I let myself be defamed? I will not yield my glory to another.
Isaiah 48:10-11

My Thoughts on Making Lemonade:

_____

_____

_____

_____

_____

_____

_____

_____

_____

_____

_____

_____

_____

_____

_____

_____

_____

_____

_____

THEY AND THEM

Have you ever noticed that when we are in a situation that seems uncomfortable, instead of taking responsibility for our actions we blame someone else? You know the ones "they" and "them." Who are they or them? The Lord will ask us where we are and what we have done, but instead of stating the facts, we always have an excuse. The Lord wants to know where we are, so we must tell Him.

Scripture: Then the man and his wife heard the sound of the Lord God as he was walking in the garden in the cool of the day, and they hid from the Lord God among the trees of the garden. But the Lord God called to the man, "Where are you?" He answered, "I heard you in the garden, and I was afraid because I was naked; so I hid." And he said, "Who told you that you were naked? Have you eaten from the tree that I commanded you not to eat from? The man said, "The woman you put here with me —she gave me some fruit from the tree, and I ate it." Then the Lord God said to the woman, "What is this you have done?" The woman said, "The serpent deceived me, and I ate."
Genesis 3:8-13

My Thoughts on Making Lemonade:

_____

_____

_____

_____

_____

_____

_____

_____

_____

_____

_____

_____

_____

_____

_____

_____

_____

_____

_____

_____

_____

_____

WISDOM

There was once an exceedingly wise king who reigned over a great nation that had two mothers who argued about the parentage of their babies. One mother had killed her own baby by sleeping on it, and she later stole the baby of the other. The mother's argued because they each claimed to be the mother of the living baby; therefore, they approached the king to solve the situation. He suggested cutting the remaining baby in half and dividing it among the two women. It was easy to identify the real mother because she would not allow such an action toward her baby. Wisdom is good judgment in a situation when you have the proper knowledge, experience and understanding.

Scripture: Get wisdom, get understanding; do not forget my words or swerve from them. Do not forsake wisdom, and she will protect you, love her, and she will watch over you. Wisdom is supreme; therefore get wisdom. Though it cost all you have, get understanding. Esteem her, and she will exalt you; embrace her, and she will honor you. She will set a garland of grace on your head and present you with a crown of splendor. Listen, my son, accept what I say, and the years of your life will be many I guide you in the way of wisdom and lead you along straight paths. When you walk, your steps will not be hampered; when you run, you will not stumble. Hold on to instruction; do not let it go; guard it well, for it is your life. Do not set foot on the path of the wicked or walk in the way of evil men. Avoid it, do not travel on it; turn from it and go on your way. **Proverbs 4:5-15**

My Thoughts on Making Lemonade:

_____

_____

_____

_____

_____

_____

_____

_____

_____

_____

_____

_____

_____

ESTHER

Many of us have self-esteem issues. We do not view ourselves as others do. We think we cannot be used to make a difference in someone's life. We are all important, and it's necessary for us to be here. There is an opportunity for you to accomplish a specific purpose. You are the only one who can do that; we are required to fulfill a specific purpose for the Lord. We have been prepared for this task. Do not look to the left or right, but look to the one that has sent you. If you don't do it, deliverance will come, but it will not come through you. You must take the attitude "the Kingdom is depending on me." It's time to sell out for the Kingdom! What have you been commanded to do?

Scripture: For if you remain silent at this time, relief and deliverance for the Jews will arise from another place, but you and your father's family will perish. And who knows but that you have come to royal position for such a time as this. **Esther 4:14**

My Thoughts for Making Lemonade:

_____

_____

_____

_____

_____

_____

_____

_____

_____

_____

_____

_____

_____

_____

_____

_____

_____

_____

_____

_____

_____

_____

_____

PURPOSE, ASSIGNMENT AND SACRIFICE

Most people think that they move through life aimlessly without direction. Everyone has had his or her steps ordered. One event in your life has a connection to other people and events in their life. We are all connected to someone and his or her purpose. As you read this devotional, we are connected by a single purpose. I may never meet you; but my assignment is fulfilled. You are required by the law of the universe to fulfill your destiny what ever it may be. You are commanded by the law of the universe to develop the gifts given to you. Your destiny may require you to sacrifice your life figuratively or literally for someone else's assignment.

Scripture: My food," said Jesus, "is to do the will of him who sent me and to finish his work. **John 4:34**

My Thoughts for Making Lemonade:

_____

_____

_____

_____

_____

41

HEARING GOD

I remember watching the movie *Beauty and the Beast* in which the Beast had to convince someone to love him while he was in his ugly state. The moment Belle said that she loved him he was changed. If we will allow God to love us, we can be changed instantly. He does not care how we look or act. He loves you. For instance, God can use a child to get a message to you if you are sensitive to the spirit. Often we miss an opportunity to hear God because we expect Him to come one particular way. God uses things to speak to us that will prick our heart. This includes tangible lessons, visuals, dreams, visions, books, and people. We must open our conscience and always measure it against the Bible, the infallible Word of God.

Scripture: I will listen to what God the Lord will say; he promises peace to his people, his saints— but let them not return to folly. Surely his salvation is near those who fear him that his glory may dwell in our land. **Psalm 85:8-9**

My Thoughts for Making Lemonade:

_____

_____

TRUCKERS

We are all familiar with truckers, individuals who drive Mack trucks, Rigs or 18-wheelers as they are often called. We are respectful of the load they carry and the distance they drive. As recipients, we are less forgiving of any complaints because we are only looking for delivery. Truck drivers are expected to have loads attached to them and for the load to be heavy, because that is what they have chosen to do. Often they will carry loads that may cause an environmental hazard if spilled. What's interesting is the trailer or the greater weight of the truck can be parked any time, leaving the trailer or weight behind. This is also true of the saints that carry unnecessary loads. We can cause an environmental hazard if we begin to spill at the wrong time and to the wrong people. God does not want us to carry a weight; he wants us to drop the load at His feet. He does not want us to carry our problems; He wants us to allow Him to work for us.

Scripture: Therefore, since we are surrounded by such a great cloud of witnesses, let us throw off everything that hinders and the sin that so easily entangles, and let us run with perseverance the race marked out for us. Let us fix our eyes on Jesus, the author and perfecter of our faith, who for the joy set before him endured the cross, scorning its shame, and sat down at the right hand of the throne of God.

Hebrews 12:1

My Thoughts for Making Lemonade:

_____

_____

_____

_____

_____

_____

_____

_____

_____

_____

_____

_____

_____

_____

_____

_____

_____

_____

_____

TWINS: THE NATURE OF MAN
The Flesh and The Spirit

While I was in the military, I worked in the labor and delivery ward of the hospital for many years. It was there we first noticed how difficult it is to tell identical twins apart. They are the mirror image of the other. They have similar personalities, and habits. As they grow and mature, they may often finish each other's sentences or feel the pain of the other when they are in distress. Twins may even confuse us by switching their own identities pretending to be the opposite one. Parents often confuse the issue by dressing twins alike. Twins have a built-in best friend. Also, they may have the same or similar habits even after being separated or never having lived together or known each other. As humans we have two natures within us, our will and the will of God. The one in charge is the one we yield ourselves to, and the other we struggle against; and to make matters worst they look similar. This is the struggle between right and wrong, good and evil.

Scripture: What shall we say, then? Is the law sin? Certainly not! Indeed I would not have known what sin was except through the law. For I would not have known what coveting really was if the law had not said, "Do not covet." But sin, seizing the opportunity afforded by the commandment, produced in me every kind of covetous desire. For apart from law, sin is dead. Once I was alive apart from law; but when the commandment came, sin sprang to life and I died. I found that the very commandment that was intended to bring life actually brought death. For sin, seizing the opportunity afforded by the commandment, deceived me, and through the commandment put me to death. So then, the law is holy, and the commandment is holy, righteous and good. Did that which is good, then, become death to me? By no means! But in order that sin might be recognized as sin, it produced death in me through what was good, so that through the commandment sin might become utterly sinful. We know that the law is spiritual; but I am unspiritual, sold as a slave to sin. I do not understand what I do. For what I want to do I do not do, but what I hate I do. And if I do what I do not want to do, I agree that the law is good. As it is, it is no longer I myself who do it, but it is sin living in me. I know that nothing good lives in me, that is, in my sinful nature. For I have the desire to do what is good, but I cannot carry it out. For what I do is not the good I want to do; no, the evil I do not want to do—this I keep on doing. Now if I do what I do not want to do, it is no longer I who do it, but it is sin living in me that does it. So I find this law at work: When I want to do good, evil is right there with me. For in my inner being I delight in God's law; but I see another law at work in the members of my body, waging war against the law of my mind and making me a prisoner of the law of sin at work within my members. What a wretched man I am! Who will rescue me from this body of death? Thanks be to God—through Jesus Christ our Lord! So then, I myself in my mind am a slave to God's law, but in the sinful nature a slave to the law of sin. **Romans 7:7-25**

My Thoughts for Making Lemonade:

_____

_____

_____

_____

_____

_____

_____

_____

_____

_____

_____

MINISTRY OF RECONCILIATION

Many people collect and redeem coupons. Unless you have collected coupons and used them you do not know the value, savings, and benefit of coupons. Often that is the way we see people. We discard them because we do not see their intrinsic value; therefore, we believe they have no value to Christ. The coupon is the same. It has value to the retailer because it is potential money. It represents a gain to the customer when the coupon is redeemed, but a lost to the retailer if it is not used. Christ has given us the ministry of reconciliation, that is, we are able to lead others back to Christ for the redemption of their sins. In spite of what may appear at face value, there is a redemptive value in the coupon and the person.

Scripture: Therefore, if anyone is in Christ, he is a new creation; the old has gone, the new has come! All this is from God, who reconciled us to himself through Christ and gave us the ministry of reconciliation: that God was reconciling the world to himself in Christ, not counting men's sins against them. And he has committed to us the message of reconciliation. We are therefore Christ's ambassadors, as though God were making his appeal

through us. We implore you on Christ's behalf: Be
reconciled to God. **2 Corinthians 5:17-20**

My Thoughts for Making Lemonade:

_____

_____

_____

_____

_____

_____

_____

_____

_____

_____

_____

_____

_____

_____

_____

_____

_____

_____

_____

TALKING TO GOD

Talking to God is to be viewed as a conversation with a dear intimate friend. The things that are revealed to God are only told to Him. Many times we give our most intimate thoughts to those we call our best friend. The problem is we all have a best friend who has a best friend, and none of them can do anything about our situation. We have to approach God knowing that He does not judge us nor does He expect us to have all of the answers, and He rewards those that seek Him. Once we give our life to Him, He is obligated to keep us from danger and supply all of our needs according to His riches in glory.

Scripture: As she kept on praying to the Lord, Eli observed her mouth. Hannah was praying in her heart, and her lips were moving, but her voice was not heard. Eli thought she was drunk and said to her, "How long will you keep on getting drunk? Get rid of your wine." "Not so, my lord," Hannah replied, "I am a woman who is deeply troubled. I have not been drinking wine or beer; I was pouring out my soul to the Lord. Do not take your servant for a wicked woman; I have been praying here out of my great anguish and grief." Eli answered, "Go in peace, and may the God of Israel grant you what you have asked of him. **I Samuel 1:12-17**

My Thoughts for Making Lemonade:

_____

_____

_____

_____

_____

_____

_____

_____

_____

_____

_____

_____

_____

_____

_____

_____

_____

_____

_____

_____

ONESIMUS

There is an Onesimus in all of us. We have all done something we are not proud of and have suffered because of it. We may have never committed a criminal offense, but we have offended others. Most often when we have committed a crime or criminal offense or had a brush with the law, it is difficult to forgive ourselves. Even though we have been released from the physical prison, we continue to be imprisoned in an emotional prison. We think that we must continue to pay a debt, which has already been forgiven. If we are going to remain in prison why did Christ come? Christ died so that we may be free.

Scripture: Although in Christ I could be bold and order you to do what you ought to do, yet I appeal to you on the basis of love. I then, as Paul—an old man and now also a prisoner of Christ Jesus—I appeal to you for my son Onesimus, who became my son while I was in chains. Formerly he was useless to you, but now he has become useful both to you and to me. I am sending him—who is my very heart—back to you. I would have liked to keep him with me so that he could take your place in helping me while I am in chains for the gospel. But I did not want to do anything without your consent, so that any favor you do will be spontaneous and not forced. Perhaps the reason he was separated from you for a little while was that you might have him back for good— no longer as a slave, but better than a slave, as a dear brother. He is very dear to me but even dearer to you, both as a man and as a brother in the Lord. So if you consider me a partner, welcome him as you would welcome me. **Philemon 1:8-17**

My Thoughts for Making Lemonade:

_____

_____

_____

_____

_____

_____

_____

_____

_____

_____

_____

_____

_____

_____

_____

STRESS
Self Trying to Resolve Every Situation Suddenly

We all have stress sometimes. It is increased when we have to do something for the first time or when we are in fear of the unknown. Different situations create stress for different people and each person responds differently. Anytime you are in a situation that makes you feel uncomfortable, it may be the onset of stress. Ask yourself what is the worst thing that can happen? Are you in a compromising situation; are you in harm's way? We often want to take care of ourselves, but God has given the angels charge over us to help us.

Scripture: He who dwells in the shelter of the Most High will rest in the shadow of the Almighty. I will say of the Lord, "He is my refuge and my fortress, my God, in whom I trust." Surely he will save you from the fowler's snare and from the deadly pestilence. He will cover you with his feathers, and under his wings you will find refuge; his faithfulness will be your shield and rampart. You will not fear the terror of night, nor the arrow that flies by day, nor the pestilence that stalks in the darkness, nor the plague that destroys at midday. A thousand may fall at your side, ten thousand at your right hand, but it will not come near you.

Psalms 91:1-7

My Thoughts for Making Lemonade:

_____

_____

_____

_____

_____

_____

_____

_____

_____

_____

_____

_____

_____

_____

_____

_____

_____

_____

_____

_____

MENU ITEMS

Where do you fit; appetizer, entrée, dessert, drink or fast food? We all have our favorite foods and places to eat. There are some places that are so exclusive that your reservation is placed months in advance. As we look at the menu we are able to pick and choose what we want based on our appetite. We may chose an appetizer making sure it will only begin to whet the appetite for what is to come. The entrée is the main course, but we've also decided that a dessert is necessary. Desserts are so decadent that the very thought makes you drool; while the drink compliments the meal and makes everything come together. Fast food, on the other hand, is quick and delicious but not necessary nutritious. Which are you; an appetizer which is the introduction to a meal but not filling? Are you an entrée leaving others asking for more or are you fast food having no real value except to yourself and not the kingdom of God. The Word of God is like a sweet dessert, which will leave your mouth watering-looking forward to the next time.

Scripture: Therefore, rid yourselves of all malice and all deceit, hypocrisy, envy, and slander of every kind. Like newborn babies, crave pure spiritual milk, so that by it you may grow up in your salvation, now that you have tasted that the Lord is good. **I Peter 2:1**

My Thoughts for Making Lemonade:

_____

_____

_____

_____

_____

_____

_____

_____

_____

_____

_____

_____

_____

_____

_____

_____

_____

_____

WHAT IS YOUR VALUE TO THE KINGDOM?

Are you a lawyer, doctor, nurse, professional athlete, teacher, cook or housekeeper? Is one profession, skilled or non-skilled more important than the other? Which profession is the best? The next time you sleep away from home think of the person you didn't see: the housekeeper. How valuable were they to the success of your visit? For a moment that person was most valuable. God has given all of us something to do and the ability to do it well for the furtherance of the gospel of Christ. We are required by all that is holy to complete the task assigned to us. You are valuable to the Kingdom, and God wants you to succeed.

Scripture: "Again, it will be like a man going on a journey, which called his servants and entrusted his property to them. To one he gave five talents of money, to another two talents, and to another one talent, each according to his ability. Then he went on his journey. The man who had received the five talents went at once and put his money to work and gained five more. So also, the one with the two talents gained two more. But the man who had received the one talent went off, dug a hole in the ground and hid his master's money. "After a long time the master of those servants returned and settled accounts with them. The man who had received the five talents brought the other five. 'Master,' he said, 'you entrusted me with five talents. See, I have gained five more.' "His master replied, 'Well done, good and faithful servant! You have been faithful with a few things; I will put you in charge of many things. Come and share your master's happiness!' "The man with the two talents also came. 'Master,' he said, 'you entrusted me with two talents; see, I have gained two more.' "His master replied, 'Well done, good and faithful servant! You have been faithful with a few things; I will put you in charge of many things. Come and share your master's happiness!' "Then the man who had received the one talent came. 'Master,' he said, 'I knew that you are a hard man, harvesting where you have not sown and gathering where you have not scattered seed. So I was afraid and went out and hid your talent in the ground. See, here is what belongs to you.' His master replied, 'you wicked, lazy servant! So you knew that I harvest where I have not sown and gather where I have not scattered seed? Well then, you should have put my money on deposit with the bankers, so that when I returned I would have received it back with interest. Take the talent from him and give it to the one who has the ten talents. For everyone who has will be given more and he will have abundance.

Matthew 25:14-29

My Thoughts for Making Lemonade:

_____

_____

_____

_____

_____

_____

_____

_____

_____

_____

_____

_____

_____

_____

_____

_____

_____

_____

_____

CAPACITY

Capacity is determined by what you are able to embrace or handle. An eight ounce glass is not required to hold the volume required of a vase for beautiful flowers or a gallon jug. An infant is not obligated to be knowledgeable or respond the same to anything or an event like an adult. Our trials are the same. The spiritual maturity of the person determines the ability to endure the trial. One person may be required to endure an enormous mental burden such as a personal illness or losing an entire family. Someone else may suffer little setbacks. Spiritual tests require us to prove our capacity by the weight of the test. We often refer to people by their ability to go through or bear certain hardships in life. We are unable to explain how some people are able to endure hardness while the same test may seem insurmountable to someone else. God knows us too well and what we're all able to bear and will not overburden us.

Scripture: For our light and momentary troubles are achieving for us an eternal glory that far outweighs them all. So we fix our eyes not on what is seen, but on what is unseen. For what is seen is temporary, but what is unseen is eternal. **II Corinthians 4:17-18**

 My Thoughts for Making Lemonade:

A WEALTHY PLACE

The wealthy place is in your mind as well as the poor place. If you think you can, you can. You can do anything you put your mind to. You are a king, you are a queen. Do not let others define you. You were fearfully and wonderfully made by God. It does not matter what anyone else says about you. What does God say about you? You can do all things with the power of Christ operating through you.

Scripture: You let men ride over our heads; we went through fire and water, but you brought us to a place of abundance. **Psalms 66:12**

My Thoughts for Making Lemonade:

_____

_____

_____

_____

_____

_____

_____

BITTER AND SWEET

Can both fresh water and salt water flow from the same spring? Can light and darkness dwell together? Let's compare a lemon to sugar. Can the sugar ever be bitter? Can the lemon be made sweet? There may be many bitter situations we face in life, but when we add Christ into our lives it causes the bitter to become sweet. Christ wants to take the bitter things in our lives and make them sweet.

Scripture: Who is wise and understanding among you? Let him show it by his good life, by deeds done in the humility that comes from wisdom. But if you harbor bitterness envy and selfish ambition in your hearts, do not boast about it or deny the truth. Such "wisdom" does not come down from heaven but is earthly, unspiritual, and of the devil. For where you have envy and selfish ambition, there you find disorder and every evil practice. But the wisdom that comes from heaven is first of all pure; then peace-loving, considerate, submissive, full of mercy and good fruit, impartial and sincere. Peacemakers who sow in peace raise a harvest of righteousness. **James 3:13-18**.

Blessed are the peacemakers, for they will be called sons of God. **Matthew 5:9**

My Thoughts for Making Lemonade:

_____

_____

_____

_____

_____

_____

_____

_____

_____

_____

_____

_____

_____

_____

_____

_____

_____

_____

_____

_____

_____

WORDS

Our words have creative power. They can be used for ammunition or praise, but they depend on the intended target. In anger we use words as ammunition and when we are delighted-for praise. However, words are so profound that when used in jesting they still produce a harvest. Our conversation must be seasoned so that we don't say something in passing that will manifest in the future. Words are used to identify new inventions and to describe the world around us. God used His words to speak the world into existence. How do you use your words?

Scripture: From the fruit of his mouth a man's stomach is filled; with the harvest from his lips he is satisfied. The tongue has the power of life and death, and those who love it will eat its fruit. **Proverbs 18:20-21**

My Thoughts for Making Lemonade:

_____

_____

_____

_____

_____

RAIN
The result of prayer

If you are praying for rain, don't complain about the mud and slush. There are certain items that are required when we are in the rain. They include coverings, such as a raincoat, a pair of boots and an umbrella. God has given us items to wear in a storm and we need to ensure we have them in place. Therefore, if you believe God answers prayer, you should prepare to receive the answer.

Scripture: So Ahab went off to eat and drink, but Elijah climbed to the top of Carmel, bent down to the ground and put his face between his knees. Go and look toward the sea," he told his servant. And he went up and looked. "There is nothing there," he said. Seven times Elijah said, "Go back. The seventh time the servant reported, "A cloud as small as a man's hand is rising from the sea." So Elijah said, "Go and tell Ahab, 'Hitch up your chariot and go down before the rain stops you. Meanwhile, the sky grew black with clouds, the wind rose, a heavy rain came and Ahab rode off to Jezreel. **I Kings 18:42-45**

 My Thoughts for Making Lemonade:

_____

_____

_____

_____

_____

_____

_____

_____

_____

_____

_____

_____

_____

_____

_____

_____

_____

_____

_____

_____

_____

_____

DEATH

Death is an opportunity for the spirit of the natural man to travel from one dimension to another. Many times people say that they are afraid to die because they do not know who God is, and they have not accepted that death is a natural part of life. For the saints, death is moving to a reward because they know what to expect. The Lord has allowed a number of people to experience heaven and to come back and explain that "it is what it is". The love of God is so overwhelming that you do not worry about anything else except being where you are. Of course, you do see love ones and there is a heavenly choir. They have said that you are immediately consumed with the presence of God. Most who have experienced heaven and who were able to articulate it did not want to return to their earthly body. To experience heaven you must die at the set time established by God.

Scripture: Give thanks to God. For none of us lives to himself alone and none of us dies to himself alone. If we live, we live to the Lord; and if we die, we die to the Lord. So, whether we live or die, we belong to the Lord. For this very reason, Christ died and returned to life so that he might be the Lord of both the dead and the living. You, then, why do you judge your brother? Or why do you look down on your brother? For we will all stand before God's judgment seat. It is written: "As surely as I live," says the Lord, "every knee will bow before me; every tongue will confess to God." So then, each of us will give an account of himself to God. **Romans 14:6-12**

My Thoughts for Making Lemonade:

_____

_____

_____

_____

_____

_____

_____

_____

_____

_____

_____

_____

_____

_____

_____

_____

_____

REMOTE CONTROL

Often we think that we are well capable of governing our lives. We do not want anyone to tell us what to do because people do not understand where we are or where we're going, and therefore they could not possibly understand us. It is considered disrespectful to just let anyone say anything to us. Our peers tell us to demand respect. They believe that people must respect us, and if they don't, we are authorized to cut them off.

I saw a movie once in which a really nice BMW was totally operated by remote control. The operator had pure enjoyment moving the car out of the enemy's way. When the enemy came near the car, the remote moved it in the opposite direction.

When we come into the knowledge of Christ, we should allow him to operate in our lives as if we were being driven by a remote control. This causes us to no longer be controlled by our circumstances, but allows the Spirit to govern us.

Scripture: So I say, live by the Spirit, and you will not gratify the desires of the sinful nature. For the sinful nature desires what is contrary to the Spirit and the Spirit what is contrary to the sinful nature. They are in conflict with each other, so that you do not do what you want. But if you are led by the Spirit, you are not under law. The acts of the sinful nature are obvious. **Galatians 5:16**

My Thoughts for Making Lemonade:

_____

_____

_____

_____

_____

_____

_____

_____

_____

_____

_____

_____

_____

_____

_____

_____

_____

_____

PICNIC

I have had the pleasure of attending several picnics in my life, and I'm always amazed with the amount of food available. There are sweets: cakes, pies, cookies and homemade ice cream. Of course I can't forget the chicken, ribs, hot dogs, burgers, fish, corn-on-the-cob, potato salad, and watermelon. Let's not forget the drinks, for children and adults. Always included are those things that make a picnic specific to a culture. This event is always designed as an opportunity to have fun and fellowship. We look for a day when the weather will be great, and if we're near the water that is an added benefit.

Because a picnic is held during the summer, we have to think of those uninvited guest such as flies, gnats, ants, rain, hot weather and sometimes cats and dogs depending on the picnics location. The event is rarely cancelled because of the attendance of the uninvited guests. God is teaching us how to trust him. There will always be situations we can't control or understand. The same way we refuse to leave the picnic because of the flies, we shouldn't leave God because of the test.

Scripture: One day the angels came to present themselves before the Lord, and Satan also came with them. The Lord said to Satan, "Where have you come from?" Satan answered the Lord, "From roaming through the earth and going back and forth in it. Then the Lord said to Satan, "Have you considered my servant Job? There is no one on earth like him; he is blameless and upright, a man who fears God and shuns evil. Does Job fear God for nothing? Satan replied. Have you not put a hedge around him and his household and everything he has? You have blessed the work of his hands, so that his flocks and herds are spread throughout the land. But stretch out your hand and strike everything he has, and he will surely curse you to your face. The Lord said to Satan, "Very well, then, everything he has is in your hands, but on the man himself do not lay a finger.

Job 1:6-12

My Thoughts for Making Lemonade:

_____

_____

_____

_____

_____

DON'T ADVERTISE THE GIFT

I have always noticed that if a merchant has a product to sell, the customer is free to handle it prior to the purchase. If it is a retail shop the customer may try the clothing on to see if it fits or if they will like how it fits them. Often if a garment is not acceptable, the person will refuse to return it to the hanger; he or she may even leave it on the floor. Because the item does not belong to them, he or she refuses to be accountable.

Likewise, in today's society young men and women like to experience the product before committing, and often this is because of the advertisement. Commercials are designed to entice the customer. Our clothing doesn't cover everything anymore. Once we have invested in great body art and it's in a preferred place we feel obligated to show it off. The tattoo artist has seen in some cases, as much as a husband. A man appreciates a woman he can respect; therefore, carry yourself as a lady so that a man will be honored to work for you as Jacob did for Rachel.

Scripture: Now Laban had two daughters; the name of the older was Leah, and the name of the younger was Rachel. Leah had weak eyes, but Rachel was lovely in form, and beautiful. Jacob was in love with Rachel and said, "I'll work for you seven years in return for your younger daughter Rachel." Laban said, "It's better that I give her to you than to some other man. Stay here with me." So Jacob served seven years to get Rachel, but they seemed like only a few days to him because of his love for her.

Genesis 29:16-20

My Thoughts for Making Lemonade:

_____
_____
_____
_____
_____
_____
_____
_____
_____
_____
_____
_____
_____
_____
_____
_____

SIN

Have you ever noticed how easy it is for smoke to cling to your clothing? Burning leaves in the fall is an exciting event, but by the end of the process your hair, clothing, and any other item close by smells of smoke. Even if you are not in the neighborhood when the fire starts, you are always made aware of its effect.

Sin is like the smoke of burning leaves. If you come to close to the leaves that are burning, you will begin to smell like smoke. Therefore, sin will cling to you, like the smell of burning leaves. Most people do not set out to sin, but the fact that they have an occasion to be around sin makes the opportunity greater. Many people who commit sin get caught up in the moment. The best chance to avoid sin is to steer clear of those things that require you to be near sin, which will leave you smelling sinful.

Scripture: For every living soul belongs to me, the father as well as the son—both alike belong to me. The soul who sins is the one who will die. **Ezekiel 18:4**

 My Thoughts for Making Lemonade:

_____

_____

_____

_____

_____

_____

_____

_____

_____

_____

_____

_____

_____

_____

_____

_____

_____

_____

_____

_____

_____

_____

TIME

Time is opportunity and a part of destiny. It is designed to establish a framework for all we are required to do. It sets the record before, during, and after events. Our life with Christ is set forth in time. He says the day you hear my voice harden not your heart. That lets us know that day is a framework. What do you do with the twenty-four hours you are given? What do you do to make a difference in the world, in your community, in your church, in your family? Have you made an impact with the time you have been given? What will the dash on your headstone mean? Have you done all the good that you can do for all the people you can. Time waits for no one and on the last day you can't tell Christ you didn't respond to what he asks because you didn't have time. Time, like faith, has been given to each of us to use as we will. What did you do with your time. Where did your time go?

Scripture: Remember how fleeting my life is. For what futility you have created all men! What man can live and not see death, or save himself from the power of the grave. **Psalms 89:47-48**

 My Thoughts for Making Lemonade:

_____

_____

_____

_____

_____

_____

_____

_____

_____

_____

_____

_____

_____

_____

_____

_____

_____

_____

_____

_____

_____

_____

_____

_____

_____

BRIDGES

A bridge is utilized to cross over obstacles. The length and span of the bridge is determined by the size of the obstacle. Some bridges can be seen in the distance, long before you reach it, you may not see others until you are upon it. Seeing the bridge in the distance is an opportunity to prepare you for the crossing. Some bridges appear luminous in the distance and are often a topic of conversation for those that have shared the experience of crossing. The glory of the bridge outweighs the obstacle it covers, usually a large body of water. Crossing the bridge is the only means of getting to the other side. Some will approach cautiously to determine how to proceed, others will move swiftly wanting the moment to pass quickly. Whatever your approach, it has to be done.

There are obstacles in our lives, and we approach them the same way we approach the bridge, some with caution and others head first, whatever the obstacle may be in your life; know that you're never alone.

Scripture: And I will ask the Father, and he will give you another Counselor to be with you forever the Spirit of truth. The world cannot accept him, because it neither sees him nor knows him. But you know him, for he lives with you and will be in you. **John 14:16**

My Thoughts for Making Lemonade:

_____

_____

_____

_____

_____

_____

_____

_____

_____

_____

_____

_____

_____

_____

_____

_____

_____

_____

CHOCOLATE

Chocolate is a delight of everyone, with its many different types and flavors. A chocolate lover is able to think of the delicacy, the taste and smell of the chocolate flood their memories. Chocolate has a profound effect on people. So much so that it is given as a sign of ones love and adoration. Chocolate can come in different forms; it can be bitter and semi-sweet. There are also so many kinds of chocolate to choose from; dark, milk and white chocolate, but to the chocoholic it is all the same. Life is much like chocolate, some days things are bitter and seems so unfair, while on other days we say life is sweet because all is well, and on those days when everything goes so well we forget to savor the moment. Events happen in our lives so that we will look to God for support. We can't live on chocolate everyday, but we need God to sustain us.

Scripture: When times are good, be happy; but when times are bad, consider: God has made the one as well as the other; therefore, a man cannot discover anything about his future. In this meaningless life of mine I have seen both of these: a righteous man perishing in his righteousness, and a wicked man living long in his wickedness. **Ecclesiastes 7:14-15**

My Thoughts for Making Lemonade:

_____

_____

_____

_____

_____

_____

_____

_____

_____

_____

_____

_____

_____

_____

_____

_____

_____

_____

_____

_____

_____

_____

WATER

Water is very fascinating! It makes up 70 percent of the planet and 70 percent of our body. It can be used to irrigate, refresh, and clean. Water has three properties: solid, liquid and gas. They all serve a different purpose. Solid ice is used to cool drinks and to make them refreshing. Solid ice may also be hail during a storm. Liquid water may be rivers, lakes and streams; liquid water may be used for washing and drinking. Water vapor, steam or gas is used to heat, cook, or provide power. The state of water may change, but water itself never changes. The same is true of Christ; He is Father, Son, and the Holy Ghost. As the Father, He is the Creator of the world and everything in it. As the Son, He is the resurrected King and Savior of the world and as the Holy Ghost; He is our in-dwelling peace, Comforter, and friend. As ice is placed in a glass to keep a drink cool and refreshing, the Holy Ghost in us will do the same, keeping us in perfect peace.

Scripture: Jesus Christ is the same yesterday and today and forever. **Hebrews 13:8**

 My Thoughts for Making Lemonade:

_____

_____

_____

_____

_____

_____

_____

_____

_____

_____

_____

_____

_____

_____

_____

_____

_____

_____

_____

_____

_____

PEACE

Peace is praying and knowing that our Eternal Father hears and answers, having confidence that He will give the response essential to the problem. Peace allows us to rest in the Word of God as if floating on a cloud.

Scripture: Keep your lives free from the love of money and be content with what you have, because God has said, "Never will I leave you; never will I forsake you." So we say with confidence, "The Lord is my helper; I will not be afraid. What can man do to me? **Hebrews 13:5.**

And the peace of God, which passeth all understanding, shall keep your hearts and minds through Christ Jesus. **Philippians 4:7**

My Thoughts for Making Lemonade:

_____

_____

_____

_____

_____

MARRIAGE

Marriage is wonderful and every girl dreams of the day she will walk down the aisle to her knight in shining armor and to experience the fulfillment of her life. She plans for this special day so that all of her friends will be there to witness the event. The young man desires to have the woman of his dreams as much as the young lady does. They are each other's best friend. They are committed to each other for a lifetime regardless of the situation. Christ is the same way. He wants to be your best friend, and he will be there forever to keep you and protect you. He will listen to all of your wild stories without judgment; He is never too busy for you.

Scripture: Remember that at that time you were separate from Christ, excluded from citizenship in Israel and foreigners to the covenants of the promise, without hope and without God in the world. But now in Christ Jesus you who once were far away have been brought near through the blood of Christ. For he himself is our peace, who has made the two one and has destroyed the barrier, the dividing wall of hostility. **Ephesians 2:12-14**

My Thoughts for Making Lemonade:

_____

_____

_____

_____

_____

_____

_____

_____

_____

_____

_____

_____

_____

_____

_____

_____

_____

_____

_____

_____

_____

CAP

Many people wear caps and some have what they will call their favorite cap. It is always in place, and the wearer would never think of leaving home without it. Everyone knows them by the cap. The observer may note how it is lovingly placed on the head and how the owner will never leave it for someone to accidentally abuse or misuse it. The cap symbolizes who the wearer is and often opens the door for conversation. It offers protection and identification. We should protect our salvation the same way. We should never allow anyone to discredit who we are in Christ. Our relationship with Christ offers identification and serves as a means to stimulate conversation.

Scripture: The Spirit of the Lord is on me, because he has anointed me to preach good news to the poor. He has sent me to proclaim freedom for the prisoners and recovery of sight for the blind, to release the oppressed, to proclaim the year of the Lord's favor. **Luke 4:18-19**

My Thoughts for Making Lemonade:

PUZZLE

Our lives are huge puzzles that are being put together everyday. The events and people in our lives contribute to the pieces. We are all connected, and every trial has a life-changing dimension attached to it. The way the situation is handled is what determines the growth or outcome of the individual. We all hold a piece of someone's puzzle. Even when we share in mundane events and activities, we don't realize we are giving a piece of the puzzle to the other person. Unless we are able to understand what the complete puzzle should be, we are unable to put the pieces together. The Lord has ordered our steps and nothing has been left to chance. The Lord is putting this puzzle together!

Scripture: For I know the plans I have for you," declares the Lord, "plans to prosper you and not to harm you, plans to give you hope and a future. Then you will call upon me and come and pray to me, and I will listen to you. You will seek me and find me when you seek me with all your heart. **Jeremiah 29:11-13**

 My Thoughts for Making Lemonade:

_____

_____

_____

_____

_____

_____

_____

_____

_____

_____

_____

_____

_____

_____

_____

_____

_____

_____

_____

_____

_____

_____

JERSEY

Have you ever noticed that people buy and wear the jersey of their favored team or athlete? The interesting thing is what they are willing to pay to own a professional jersey. Everyone is able to determine by looking at the jersey if it is a genuine shirt or not. The person may even wear the jersey over another type of clothing. Often we refer to it as a "jersey" and everyone understands that we are speaking of a professional shirt. We all want to belong and be accepted therefore, we may be pre-occupied with someone's name or logo on our clothing and often refer to the item by the brand.

How is it we can wear the shirt of a man who has never done anything for us or that we will never meet, but we are ashamed of Christ who died for us? We refuse to let anyone know that we love Jesus. Just as we are willing to wear a jersey to show who we represent, we should also be willing to make others aware of whom we serve so we won't miss opportunities to witness to our friends.

Scripture: I am not ashamed of the gospel, because it is the power of God for the salvation of everyone who believes: first for the Jew, then for the Gentile. For in the gospel the righteousness from God is revealed, a righteousness that is by faith from first to last, just as it is written: "The righteous will live by faith. **Romans 1:16-17**

My Thoughts for Making Lemonade:

_____

_____

_____

_____

_____

_____

_____

_____

_____

_____

_____

_____

_____

_____

_____

_____

_____

_____

MY FIVE

We are all familiar with the terms caller ID, my five, roll over minutes, dropped calls, dead zones, I have my people with me, friends, and family plans. All of these terms let us know how close we are to the other person. This determination lets us know how important or insignificant we are to his or her life. The position we hold explains our level of prominence in his or her life. Christ has a caller ID because He is expecting us to call. He has us in his five because we are His favorite, and our calls are never dropped because there are no dead zones since His people are always working. We are His friends, and the family plan is glorious!

Scripture: Keep your lives free from the love of money and be content with what you have because God has said, "Never will I leave you; never will I forsake you. So we say with confidence, "The Lord is my helper; I will not be afraid. What can man do to me?" **Hebrews 13:5-6**

My Thoughts for Making Lemonade:

HIT THE WALL

It's incredible that some of us will know that something is bad for us, but we continue to move towards the negativity even as the warnings are given. One inner voice says to go ahead it will not happen to you, and the other voice is giving warnings and examples. Some people will learn by watching others while some will hear the warning and get the message. Most of us will have to experience the lesson. Of course none is better than the other; however, one does not have to experience a situation to learn a life-changing lesson. After we hit the wall, we may learn the lesson, but for some it has to be rock bottom before we realize that there is a power much greater than any we have ever encountered.

Scripture: But God did say, 'You must not eat fruit from the tree that is in the middle of the garden, and you must not touch it, or you will die." "You will not surely die," the serpent said to the woman. "For God knows that when you eat of it your eyes will be opened, and you will be like God, knowing good and evil." When the woman saw that the fruit of the tree was good for food and pleasing to the eye, and also desirable, for gaining wisdom, she took some and ate it. She also gave some to her husband, who was with her, and he ate it. Then the eyes of both of them were opened, and they realized they were naked. **Genesis 3:3-7**

My Thoughts for Making Lemonade:

_____

_____

_____

_____

_____

_____

_____

_____

_____

_____

_____

_____

_____

_____

_____

_____

_____

_____

CAKE

Everyone enjoys a mouthwatering slice of cake every once in a while, but we never consider the process that each individual ingredient had to go through before it was considered for the cake. We don't think about a chicken being denied parenthood to give six eggs, or a cow needing to give birth to a calf just to produce milk for cream or butter. We don't consider that stalks of sugarcane have to be pressed to extract the juice which produces sugar. These items are necessary to produce one cake. Of course during the mixing process some things are beaten, some are separated, others are mixed, and heat is added for a specific period of time. The outcome of this process is delicious. Isn't it amazing we call it "done" when a cake has finished baking? Everyone loves the flavor of a great cake. During the course of our Christian walk, we will have some of the same experiences; separating, beating, pressing, and heating. The question is: Are you done?

Scripture: See, I have refined you, though not as silver; I have tested you in the furnace of affliction. For my own sake, for my own sake, I do this. How can I let myself be defamed? I will not yield my glory to another. **Isaiah 48:10**

My Thoughts for Making Lemonade:

RESTAURANT

Think of your favorite restaurant and how you enjoy going there. You have a clear idea of the entrée you will enjoy and can almost taste it as you speak of it. You're able to have your preferred waitress or waiter, and they are so familiar with you that they are able to determine your order. Christ wants to have the same relationship with you. He wants to anticipate you coming to talk to Him although He already knows what you want; therefore, He is ready and prepared to give you whatever you are requesting.

Scripture: "So I say to you: Ask and it will be given to you; seek and you will find; knock and the door will be opened to you. For everyone who asks receives; he who seeks finds; and to him who knocks, the door will be opened. **Luke 11:9-10**

My Thoughts for Making Lemonade:

_____

_____

_____

_____

_____

CAR

We all have our favorite car and enjoy explaining to our friends exactly how it looks and how fast it may go. We love the gadgets; such as a navigational system, cruise, remote start, heated seats and windows, lane departure signals as well as a rear camera backup system. The Holy Ghost is the same. He is our navigational system; He is the remote start and heated windows. Most importantly, He will let you know when you have departed the lane. Because He is our comforter; He will never leave nor forsake us, He wants us to cruise in the spirit.

Scripture: And I will ask the Father, and he will give you another Counselor to be with you forever— the Spirit of truth. The world cannot accept him, because it neither sees him nor knows him. But you know him, for he lives with you and will be in you. **John 14:16**

My Thoughts for Making Lemonade:

_____

_____

_____

BABY'S DADDY

There is a term that is common today called "my baby's daddy." This term originated to define the seed donor of a young girl's baby when the baby's father does not have a relationship with the mother. In some cases, the father does not have any dealing with the baby either. Often prior to and after pregnancy, the baby's father makes a promise to the young lady he is unable to keep. God always keeps His promises. He is our Father not our "baby daddy."

Scripture: When Judah saw her, (Tamar) he thought she was a prostitute, for she had covered her face. Not realizing that she was his daughter-in-law, he went over to her by the roadside and said, "Come now, let me sleep with you. "And what will you give me to sleep with you?" she asked. I'll send you a young goat from my flock," he said. "Will you give me something as a pledge until you send it?" she asked. He said, "What pledge should I give you?" "Your seal and its cord, and the staff in your hand," she answered. So he gave them to her and slept with her, and she became pregnant by him. After she left, she took off her veil and put on her widow's clothes again. Meanwhile Judah sent the young goat by his friend the Adullamite in order to get his pledge back from the woman, but he did not find her.

106

He asked the men who lived there, "Where is the shrine prostitute who was beside the road at Enaim?" "There hasn't been any shrine prostitute here," they said. So he went back to Judah and said, "I didn't find her. Besides, the men who lived there said, 'There hasn't been any shrine prostitute here.' Then Judah said, "Let her keep what she has, or we will become a laughingstock. After all, I did send her this young goat, but you didn't find her." About three months later Judah was told, "Your daughter-in-law Tamar is guilty of prostitution, and as a result she is now pregnant." Judah said, "Bring her out and have her burned to death!" As she was being brought out, she sent a message to her father-in-law. "I am pregnant by the man who owns these," she said. And she added, "See if you recognize whose seal and cord and staff these are." Judah recognized them and said, "She is more righteous than I, since I wouldn't give her to my son Selah.

Genesis 38:15-26.

 My Thoughts for Making Lemonade:

_____

_____

_____

EVIL PLANS

Often we will say things without thinking in an attempt to be cute or clever; but God is listening to everything that we're saying and will require us to give an account of those things spoken in jest. A fool says foolish things and in his mind he plans evil. A fool does things that are wicked and says wrong things about the Lord. Don't think about planning evil against or speaking evil against your brother.

Scripture: For the fool speaks folly, his mind is busy with evil: He practices ungodliness and spreads error concerning the Lord, the hungry he leaves empty and from the thirsty he withholds water. The scoundrel's methods are wicked, he makes up evil schemes. **Isaiah 32:6-7**

My Thoughts for Making Lemonade:

_____

_____

_____

_____

_____

_____

GRACE AND MERCY

We are all enemies of the cross, but because of who Christ is, he died so that we could inherit the Kingdom of God. Now just what is mercy and why should it be extended? We have all committed immoral behaviors of which we're not proud. For some we should have been placed in prison. Christ, in His love and wisdom, has His hand on us from the foundation of the earth and has already claimed us for the Kingdom. He became our lawyer and pleads our cases before the enemy, exonerating us, and giving us an opportunity to live eternally in Heaven; therefore mercy is favor, leniency, and the blessing of the Lord. Because of Christ's death we can inherit the Kingdom of God.

Scripture: But because of his great love for us, God, who is rich in mercy, made us alive with Christ even when we were dead in transgressions—it is by grace you have been saved. And God raised us up with Christ and seated us with him in the heavenly realms in Christ Jesus, in order that in the coming ages he might show the incomparable riches of his grace, expressed in his kindness to us in Christ Jesus. For it is by grace you have been saved, through faith—and this not from yourselves, it is the gift of God—not by works, so that no one can boast. **Ephesians 2:4-9**

My Thoughts for Making Lemonade:

_____

_____

_____

_____

_____

_____

_____

_____

_____

_____

_____

_____

_____

_____

_____

_____

_____

GANGS

Everyone wants to be accepted and to be a part of something successful. We place value on how well we may be received into a group and as little children we want to be chosen first for games instead of last. Last says that we aren't wanted and may not be the best person for the part. Some people join gangs, fraternities, sororities or clubs because they identify with the groups' thinking and principles. We wear our colors, create our signs, and sing our songs to identify us. Schools have mascots that represent power and prestige. Some schools are recognized entirely by the mascot. Christ is the same way; He accepts us into the kingdom, and it doesn't matter to him if we are weak or frail because He said "in our weakness he will make us strong." Jesus traveled with twelve of his closest friends making a difference in the world. They were recognized as his disciples or followers. Wherever He went, He made a difference. He healed the sick, raised the dead, fed the hungry and turned water into wine. When you're with your friends what are you doing?

Scripture: Jesus' brothers said to him, "You ought to leave here and go to Judea, so that your disciples may see the miracles you do. No one who wants to become a public figure acts in secret. Since you are doing these things, show yourself to the world." For even his own brothers did not believe in him. Therefore Jesus told them, "The right time for me has not yet come; for you any time is right. The world cannot hate you, but it hates me because I testify that what it does is evil. **John 7:3-7**

My Thoughts for Making Lemonade:

_____

_____

_____

_____

_____

_____

_____

_____

_____

_____

_____

_____

_____

_____

_____

_____

SALVATION

We think that we're in control of our lives but that is contrary to the truth. Our steps are ordered by the Lord and nothing happens by chance. Every event and opportunity; disappointing or otherwise is to prepare us for the Kingdom. Salvation brings deliverance, security, recovery, escape, health and peace. Without Christ, we are always looking for answers for problems, but our strength is limited in crucial situations. There are positions in which we may find ourselves, and it is impossible for those that are close to us to help. The answer for all our questions is within Christ.

Scripture: But what does it say? "The word is near you; it is in your mouth and in your heart," that is, the word of faith we are proclaiming: That if you confess with your mouth, "Jesus is Lord," and believe in your heart that God raised him from the dead, you will be saved. For it is with your heart that you believe and are justified, and it is with your mouth that you confess and are saved.
Romans 10:8-10

My Thoughts for Making Lemonade:

_____

_____

_____

_____

_____

_____

_____

_____

_____

_____

_____

_____

_____

_____

_____

_____

_____

_____

_____

_____

_____

MAKE-UP

Make-up is used for a number of reasons; in theater it gives the *actor* the personality and look needed to portray a particular character. It can be used to *conceal* flaws one may think they have in their personal features, and it is used to *enhance* the given beauty of a person. We are no more than actors when we try to conceal our imperfections from Christ, and He gave his life so that we would have beauty for ashes.

Scripture: He has sent me to bind up the brokenhearted, to proclaim freedom for the captives and release from darkness for the prisoners, to proclaim the year of the Lord's favor and the day of vengeance of our God, to comfort all who mourn, and provide for those who grieve in Zion—to bestow on them a crown of beauty instead of ashes, the oil of gladness instead of mourning, and a garment of praise instead of a spirit of despair. They will be called oaks of righteousness, a planting of the Lord for the display of his splendor. **Isaiah 61:1-3**

 My Thoughts for Making Lemonade:

_____

_____

_____

_____

_____

_____

_____

_____

_____

_____

_____

_____

_____

_____

_____

_____

_____

_____

_____

_____

_____

_____

GONE FISHING

Fishing is a huge sport and many anglers are rewarded thousands of dollars for the prized catch. When the angler goes out, he is already aware of what he plans to catch and why. He may spend hours on a boat waiting for a bite, but he is patient. The strategy is to use proper bait. Christ has called us to be fishers of men. We should cast out our nets to draw men to Christ. We have to use wisdom and be willing to follow his instructions, especially when choosing bait.

Scripture: "I'm going out to fish," Simon Peter told them, and they said, "We'll go with you." So they went out and got into the boat, but that night they caught nothing. Early in the morning, Jesus stood on the shore, but the disciples did not realize that it was Jesus. He called out to them, "Friends haven't you any fish?" "No," they answered. He said, "Throw your net on the right side of the boat and you will find some." When they did, they were unable to haul the net in because of the large number of fish. **John 21:3-6**

My Thoughts for Making Lemonade:

FRIENDS

We all have dear friends that if we were in trouble we would only need to give them a call, and they would be there in a hurry. Now of course it doesn't matter if you're right or wrong because a real friend loves at all times. They protect your back, but tell you the truth. A real friend doesn't require you to apologize for the little mistakes. A real friend will always allow you to be yourself knowing that he or she will love you in spite of your shortcomings. They don't love because of who you are, but in spite of who you are. If you have true friends, treasure them because many do not.

Scripture: A friend loves at all times, and a brother is born for adversity. **Proverbs 17:17**

My Thoughts for Making Lemonade:

_____

_____

_____

_____

_____

FAMILY

A family is the unit of people God has given to keep us grounded. He has given us the structure father, mother and children. The father is to provide provisions and safety in the home while the mother establishes order and character. The children are to obey the parents so that they may have long lives. Our current moral culture has eroded this system. The father is no longer in the home to provide protection; therefore, the safety of the daughters is compromised. The boys are not being led to manhood by the father; therefore, he does not respect the women in his life. When this happens, the daughter is neglected. This means children are being raised without boundaries; therefore; they can do whatever they please. The parents are preoccupied with life. To successfully reclaim our community and children, the spirit of family has to be reintroduced to our society.

Scripture: We have a young sister, and her breasts are not yet grown. What shall we do for our sister for the day she is spoken for? If she is a wall, we will build towers of silver on her. If she is a door, we will enclose her with panels of cedar. **Song of Solomon 8:8**

 My Thoughts for Making Lemonade:

_____

_____

_____

_____

_____

_____

_____

_____

_____

_____

_____

_____

_____

_____

_____

_____

_____

_____

_____

_____

_____

_____

FIRE FLIES

How often have you seen a summer firefly and attempted to catch it to no avail? This reminds you of a carefree time, a time of freedom, and joy. When you do catch one, you can place it on your clothing, and it will glow in the dark for a period of time. The excitement of capturing the insect and knowing that your friends could see you from across the yard is an experience shared by participants.

Christ wants to capture us and place us in His heart and have us glow for Him, therefore we will be a light for Him in a dying world.

Scripture: You are the light of the world. A city on a hill cannot be hidden. Neither do people light a lamp and put it under a bowl. Instead they put it on its stand, and it gives light to everyone in the house. In the same way, let your light shine before men, that they may see your good deeds and praise your Father in heaven. **Matthew 5:15-16**

 My Thoughts for Making Lemonade:

LOSS

Loss for some is relief for others, or disbelief and a pain that's deep. If you have never lost a friend, a family member or pet you would not have a clear understanding of what "loss" means. Some things are counted lost if we misplace them because we are simply careless. Others may be lost because time has expired on a relationship caused by time or death; however, it is all the same. There is emptiness in your heart because of the missing piece. You long for the person or pet knowing that they can't come to you. Accepting the reality of the pain is the beginning of healing. Christ wants to fill any emptiness in our hearts when we are able to return to a routine that does not include the lost one.

Scripture: After the boy had gone, David got up from the south side of the stone and bowed down before Jonathan three times, with his face to the ground. Then they kissed each other and wept together—but David wept the most. Jonathan said to David, "Go in peace, for we have sworn friendship with each other in the name of The Lord, saying, The Lord is witness between you and me, and between your descendants and my descendants forever." Then David left, and Jonathan went back to the town. **I Samuel 20:41-42**

My Thoughts for Making Lemonade:

_____

_____

_____

_____

_____

_____

_____

_____

_____

_____

_____

_____

_____

_____

_____

_____

_____

_____

_____

_____

_____

_____

LIE

To lie is to fabricate a sequence of events so realistic or bizarre that even the storyteller is able to believe it. To lie is to create an environment so believable that it protects the liar from the real truth or his actions or the consequences of his actions. A lie is intended to deceive someone intentionally so that he or she is unable to discern the truth. A lie is designed to protect the liar from the current facts or reality that he or she is unable to hear and appreciate. Sometimes the liar will lie to "protect someone." The lie creates a buffer from a world that may be too harsh, and it buys time for the liar. A lie can create an entire new reality for the liar. Christ encourages us not to lie to one another.

Scripture: Do not lie to each other, since you have taken off your old self with its practices and have put on the new self, which is being renewed in knowledge in the image of its Creator. **Colossians 3:9-10**

My Thoughts for Making Lemonade:

MALE CHILD

The male child is the pride of any single mother's life. She refers to him as her little man, dresses him as a man and allows him to behave as a man would, but she never reminds him that he is a *man-in-training*. She does not teach him to love God so that he will love and respect her and other women. She does not explain that a man cares for and will give his life for his family. She does not explain to him that it is not good to touch a woman unless she is his wife. She does not explain to him that God has asked him to provide and protect the house. She does not tell him that his woman is a queen and should be respected as one.

Scripture: The sayings of King Lemuel—an oracle his mother taught him: O my son, O son of my womb, O son of my vows, do not spend your strength on women, your vigor on those who ruin kings. Speak up for those who cannot speak for themselves, for the rights of all who are destitute. Speak up and judge fairly; defend the rights of the poor and needy. **Proverbs 31:1-3, 8-9**

My Thoughts for Making Lemonade:

_____

_____

_____

_____

_____

_____

_____

_____

_____

_____

_____

_____

_____

_____

_____

_____

_____

_____

_____

_____

_____

_____

FEMALE CHILD

She is the love of his life, beautiful and tender in his sight. Her innocence forever protected by him. She is his angel. She is being protected and provided for because he gave his word. Her trust is in him because she knows that she has value. He will not hurt or betray her. He will never leave or forsake her. Who is she: your mother, your sister, your wife, your niece and your aunt?

Scripture: We have a young sister, and her breasts are not yet grown. What shall we do for our sister for the day she is spoken for? If she is a wall, we will build towers of silver on her. If she is a door, we will enclose her with panels of cedar. **Song of Solomon 8:8-9**

My Thoughts for Making Lemonade:

_____

_____

_____

_____

_____

_____

_____

LOVE

What is love and how do we define it? We often use the term "love" to define how we feel about shoes, food, cars, clothes and movies. To love is to have a relationship with something. How can we have a relationship with any object? Defining love by possessions means that we have a narrow view of our world and surroundings. Love is a growing maturity with those we care most about. We can allow them to be themselves without fear of judgment. Love does not demand that others conform to our views or desires. Love is allowing me to be me, and accepting my imperfections knowing that through God I am perfect. God is love.

Scripture: If I speak in the tongues of men and of angels, but have not love, I am only a resounding gong or a clanging cymbal. If I have the gift of prophecy and can fathom all mysteries and all knowledge, and if I have a faith that can move mountains, but have not love, I am nothing. If I give all I possess to the poor and surrender my body to the flames, but have not love, I gain nothing. Love is patient, love is kind. It does not envy, it does not boast, it is not proud. It is not rude, it is not self-seeking, it is not easily angered, it keeps no record of wrongs. Love does not delight in evil but rejoices with the truth. It always protects, always trusts, always hopes; always perseveres. Love never fails. But where there are prophecies, they will cease; where there are tongues, they will be stilled; where there is knowledge, it will pass away. For we know in part and we prophesy in part, but when perfection comes, the imperfect disappears. When I was a child, I talked like a child I thought like a child, I reasoned like a child. When I became a man, I put childish ways behind me. Now we see but a poor reflection as in a mirror; then we shall see face to face. Now I know in part; then I shall know fully, even as I am fully known. And now these three remain: faith, hope and love. But the greatest of these is love.

I Corinthians 13:1-13

My Thoughts for Making Lemonade:

_____

_____

_____

_____

_____

_____

FRUIT TREES

Trees are definitely known by their fruit. I have seen pear, orange, grapefruit and fig trees, and they all produce their own fruit. There is never an opportunity to pick one fruit from another type of tree. We are also fruit trees, and we bear the fruit of our nature. If we are sweet, kind, and considerate, then of course our fruit is the same. If we are deceitful, manipulative, and evil then of course our fruit will bear the same. Every now and then we all need to check our fruit.

Scripture: Likewise every good tree bears good fruit, but a bad tree bears bad fruit. A good tree cannot bear bad fruit, and a bad tree cannot bear good fruit. Every tree that does not bear good fruit is cut down and thrown into the fire. Thus, by their fruit you will recognize them.
Matthew 7:17-20

My Thoughts for Making Lemonade:

_____

_____

_____

134

CRUISE CONTROL

Many years ago a car didn't come with cruise control; therefore, if we were traveling a great distance we had to keep our foot on the gas and attempt to keep the car at the established posted speed. Today, cars are routinely equipped with cruise control and as a driver we can program the car to travel at the desired speed. If we should encounter an obstacle, we have a choice to take the cruise off or touch the breaks and resume the set speed when the obstacle passes. The Holy Ghost within us is the same way; it is set at a given speed according to the destination where God is leading. If we encounter an obstacle we can choose to handle it ourselves or allow the Holy Ghost to slow us down and resume the set speed when the obstacle passes.

Scripture: But you will receive power when the Holy Spirit comes on you; and you will be my witnesses in Jerusalem, and in all Judea and Samaria, and to the ends of the earth. **Acts 1:8**

My Thoughts for Making Lemonade:

STAINS

There are several commercial items on the market that can be utilized to remove stains from our clothing. "Tide Stick" and "Spray and Wash" both provide an excellent service. When it comes to the removal of sin that we have accumulated over the years, it takes the blood of Jesus to wash it away.

Scripture: He is dressed in a robe dipped in blood, and his name is the Word of God. **Revelation 19:13**

My Thoughts on Making Lemonade:

_____

_____

_____

_____

_____

_____

_____

_____

_____

_____

CPR

Cardiopulmonary Resuscitation (CPR) is an opportunity to give someone life after that person has died suddenly. If the procedure is effective, the individual will regain life and live a normal healthy life afterwards. Prior to having a relationship with Christ, we were dead and unaware that we needed to be revived again, but Christ, who loved us and gave His life for us, has given us an opportunity to be the living among the dead.

Scripture: As for you, you were dead in your transgressions and sins, in which you used to live, when you followed the ways of this world and of the ruler of the kingdom of the air, the spirit who is now at work in those who are disobedient. All of us also lived among them at one time, gratifying the cravings of our sinful nature and following its desires and thoughts. Like the rest, we were by nature objects of wrath. But because of his great love for us, God, who is rich in mercy, made us alive with Christ even when we were dead in transgressions--it is by grace you have been saved. **Ephesians 2:1-5**

My Thoughts for Making Lemonade:

_____

_____

_____

_____

_____

_____

_____

_____

_____

_____

_____

_____

_____

_____

_____

_____

_____

_____

_____

_____

_____

_____

G.P.S.

The Global Positioning System (GPS) is precise. It identifies location and time information anywhere on or near the earth to determine directions to unfamiliar areas or destinations. In order to use it, you will have to program the desired location into the computer, and the navigational system will give you turn by turn directions to the location. We as a people trust these devices more than we trust the Holy Ghost when, the Holy Ghost is a Spiritual Navigational System. Lack of understanding and trust make us lean to our own understanding, but when we become lost, we must look to the Lord.

Scripture: Trust in the Lord with all your heart and lean not to your own understanding in all your ways acknowledge him and he will direct your path. **Proverbs 3:5-6**

My Thoughts for Making Lemonade:

_____

_____

_____

_____

UMBRELLA

We view an umbrella as insignificant when it is not needed. The purpose of the umbrella is to provide protection in the event of inclement weather. We do not carry it all the time, but most people own one, and it's always available. In an emergency we know how to find it and use it. Prayer is like an umbrella. We don't use it all the time, but it provides protection and covers us in a storm. It's always available, and in an emergency we know how to find it and use it.

Scripture: And pray in the Spirit on all occasions. **Ephesians 6:18a**

In the same way, the Spirit helps us in our weakness. We do not know what we ought to pray for, but the Spirit himself intercedes for us with groans that words cannot express. And he who searches our hearts knows the mind of the Spirit, because the Spirit intercedes for the saints in accordance with God's will. **Romans 8:26-27**

My Thoughts for Making Lemonade:

CPU

The Central Processing Unit (CPU) is the main component of the computer. If the information is going to be processed, it has to pass through the unit. Software installed on the system will identify any program that is faulty or illegal. It will let you know when you need to upgrade your device based on a preset identifier in the unit. Christ is the same way. He knows what we have need of, and will give us different tests when we need to be upgraded, or our capacity needs to be increased.

Scripture: For I know the plans I have for you," declares the Lord, "plans to prosper you and not to harm you, plans to give you hope and a future. **Jeremiah 29:11**

My Thoughts for Making Lemonade:

_____

_____

_____

_____

_____

_____

CHURCH

We often think that going to church is all that we need to fulfill the requirement God has given us to be fruitful and multiply. He has called us to be seed for the sower and bread for the hungry. However, if we never become the seed, how can anyone be fed? The assembling of ourselves together provides an opportunity for us to be refreshed. Christ is calling us to be our brothers' keeper and labors in the Kingdom.

Scripture: All the believers were together and had everything in common. Selling their possessions and goods, they gave to anyone as he had need. Every day they continued to meet together in the temple courts. They broke bread in their homes and ate together with glad and sincere hearts, praising God and enjoying the favor of all the people. And the Lord added to their number daily those who were being saved. **Acts 2:44-47**

My Thoughts for Making Lemonade:

_____

_____

WHAT'S IN A NAME?

What's in a name really depends on who you are and what the name may mean to the public. If we see a "bucket" in the sky our minds immediately think of Kentucky Fried Chicken, two "Golden Arches" could be McDonalds and if you say, "Be like Mike," many may think that you might be speaking of Michael Jordan. It is safe to say that a reputation is staked on a name and that reputation is built by the confidence one has in it. There are some that are known by one name such as Oprah, Cleopatra, Madonna, Obama and Jesus. Your name is all you have, and your reputation is built on your name.

Scripture: Therefore God exalted him to the highest place and gave him the name that is above every name, that at the name of Jesus every knee should bow, in heaven and on earth and under the earth, and every tongue confess that Jesus Christ is Lord, to the glory of God the Father. **Philippians 2:9-11**

 My Thoughts for Making Lemonade:

THE KNOCK

Doors represent opportunity, and it is entirely up to the individual to seize the moment. People, moments, and incidents all represent the door. Often we are unaware of the timing in the spirit because we are unaware of the movement of Christ. If we become more sensitive to the spirit, we will be able to hear the knock.

Scripture: Here I am! I stand at the door and knock. If anyone hears my voice and opens the door, I will come in and eat with him, and he with me. To him who overcomes, I will give the right to sit with me on my throne, just as I overcame and sat down with my Father on his throne. He, who has an ear, let him hear what the Spirit says to the churches. **Revelation 3:20-22**

My Thoughts for Making Lemonade:

_____

_____

_____

_____

_____

WINE

Wine is a beverage made of the fermented juice of various kinds of fruit or plants and used for entertainment. When living or visiting over seas, people are often told to drink the wine because the water is unhealthy. When Jesus was given water, he turned it into wine. God is able to take whatever we present him and turn into something that represents His power and authority. We must be mindful that we do not desire His glory and authority or take it for ourselves. He is able to make the weak strong,

Scripture: On the third day a wedding took place at Cana in Galilee. Jesus' mother was there, and Jesus and his disciples had also been invited to the wedding. When the wine was gone, Jesus' mother said to him, "They have no more wine." "Dear woman, why do you involve me?" Jesus replied. "My time has not yet come." His mother said to the servants, "Do whatever he tells you." Nearby stood six stone water jars, the kind used by the Jews for ceremonial washing, each holding from twenty to thirty gallons. Jesus said to the servants, "Fill the jars with water;" so they filled them to the brim. Then he told them, "Now draw some out and take it to the master of the banquet." They did so, and the master of the banquet tasted the water that had been turned into wine. He did not realize where it had come from, though the servants who had drawn the water knew. Then he called the bridegroom aside and said, "Everyone brings out the choice wine first and then the cheaper wine after the guests have had too much to drink; but you have saved the best till now." This, the first of his miraculous signs, Jesus performed at Cana in Galilee. He thus revealed his glory, and his disciples put their faith in him. **John 2:1-11**

Wine is a mocker and beer a brawler; whoever is led astray by them is not wise. **Proverbs 20:1**

It is not for kings, O Lemuel— not for kings to drink wine, not for rulers to crave beer, lest they drink and forget what the law decrees, and deprive all the oppressed of their rights. **Proverbs 31:4-5**

 My Thoughts for Making Lemonade:

_____

_____

_____

ANGEL OF HOPE

Have you ever had an opportunity to be the angel of hope for someone? Have you ever had the opportunity to be in the right place, at the right time, to say the right thing to the right person, for the right reason? There are hurting people all around us and often we as saints pass by them without so much as a second look. I remember an opportunity I had recently in a restaurant when the server had what I thought was a bad attitude. When I stopped to look in her face, I saw the pain and had to repent and offer her hope in Christ. We are the answer.

Scripture: I eagerly expect and hope that I will in no way be ashamed, but will have sufficient courage so that now as always Christ will be exalted in my body, whether by life or by death. For to me, to live is Christ and to die is gain. If I am to go on living in the body, this will mean fruitful labor for me. **Philippians 1:20-22**

Let your light so shine before men, that they may see your good works, and glorify your Father which is in heaven. **Matthew 5:16**

 My Thoughts for Making Lemonade:

_____

_____

_____

_____

_____

_____

_____

_____

_____

_____

_____

_____

_____

_____

_____

_____

_____

_____

_____

_____

_____

_____

VIRGIN DRINKS

Before accepting Christ, many of us went to the club and would order virgin drinks. We wanted to fit in with the group without having to explain ourselves. As Christians that is not an option. We are to drink the cup given to us so that others may see and have hope. It may appear to be easier to drink the cup of others sometime until we realize the suffering offered with their cup. Everyone has been equipped to drink of his or her own cup. We will never have more than we can bear, and *we are the witness* for the cup we drink.

Scripture: Can you drink the cup I drink or be baptized with the baptism I am baptized with? **Mark 10:38.**

My Thoughts for Making Lemonade:

_____

_____

_____

_____

_____

_____

SHOES

How often do you tell someone you "love" their shoes, but did you ever stop to think how much they had to pay for the shoes that they wear? Shoes represent your walk, your direction and circumstances. Will you walk a mile in someone else's shoes? The next time you want to criticize or judge, walk in the shoes of another. Everything is spiritual. Our steps are ordered, and the place we stand is Holy Ground because it is our ordained walk.

Scripture: Then the Lord said to him, 'Take off your sandals; the place where you are standing is holy ground. **Acts 7:33**

Thoughts for Making Lemonade:

_____

_____

_____

_____

_____

_____

_____

MOSS and KUDZU

When one lives in the South one has an opportunity to witness numerous unique things; two of them being moss and kudzu. Both are plants that receive their life substance from another tree or plant, and both will take over the item of attachment. Kudzu will completely engulf the tree, trunk included, while moss will live on the branches and leaves. They never attach to anything that is dead; sin is the same way. Some sins will completely take over to the point we are not recognizable while others will take over but leave just enough of you exposed to be identifiable; however, Christ has come to remove the sin from our lives so that we become dead and become more like Him.

Scripture: The thief comes only to steal and kill and destroy; I have come that they may have life, and have it to the full. **John 10:10**.

 My Thoughts for Making Lemonade:

_____

_____

BABY

Babies are a gift from God and an indication of how we are to trust Him in all that we do. Babies rely totally on the caregiver. They are not concerned about anything; they trust the person responsible for providing care. They do not ask questions, they are not concerned about what they are going to eat or wear, and they just rest. The Lord wants us to trust Him and rest.

Scripture: I am still confident of this: I will see the goodness of the Lord in the land of the living. Wait for the Lord, be strong and take heart and wait for the Lord. **Psalms 27:13-14.**

Therefore I tell you, do not worry about your life, what you will eat or drink; or about your body, what you will wear. Is not life more important than food, and the body more important than clothes? Look at the birds of the air; they do not sow or reap or store away in barns, and yet your heavenly Father feeds them. Are you not much more valuable than they? Who of you by worrying can add a single hour to his life? And why do you worry about clothes? See how the lilies of the field grow. They do not labor or spin. Yet I tell you that not even Solomon in all his

splendor was dressed like one of these. If that is how God clothes the grass of the field, which is here today and tomorrow is thrown into the fire, will he not much more clothe you, O you of little faith? So do not worry, saying, 'What shall we eat?" or 'What shall we drink?' or 'What shall we wear?' For the pagans run after all these things, and your heavenly Father knows that you need them.
Matthew 6:25-32

My Thoughts for Making Lemonade:

_____

_____

_____

_____

_____

_____

_____

_____

_____

_____

_____

_____

_____

STORMS

Recently while on a trip to Florida there was a really bad rainstorm, the lights flickered, the lighting struck and the wind blew. Although the lights never went out, we turned all of the lights off and began to use candles and lamps in anticipation of the lights going out. We began to take matters into our own hands based on past experience and our own abilities. This storm only lasted an hour, but because we did not know the outcome, and anticipated the intensity to be great; we were fearful. The storms of life only come to increase our faith; it doesn't matter the force because God wants us to trust Him and not make provisions for ourselves.

Scripture: He replied, "You of little faith, why are you so afraid?" Then he got up and rebuked the winds and the waves, and it was completely calm. **Matthew 8:26**

My Thoughts for Making Lemonade:

_____

_____

_____

SPIRIT OF CONTROL

There are a number of "spirits." Some include manipulation and control. In fact, we are servants to anyone or anything outside of ourselves that we allow to give direction to us through domination, manipulation or mind-control. For instance, in our peer group we are led by the strongest personality. We may do any and everything our peer group suggests, not thinking for ourselves. Even when that person is not physically there we continue to yield to the same directions. Sometimes in a male-female, or female-male relationship one person will check the phone of the other friend or ask personal questions about their whereabouts when they are apart. This is different from the married relationship when the spouses are accountable to each other. The spirit becomes so oppressive that when individuals have broken free, they still behave as if they are being controlled. We are not to be controlled. We are to be loved and trusted. If we love something we should let it go because if it is ours it will return to us. Love is free to be yourself. Satan does the same thing. We allow him to control us for so long that when we are set free, we fail to move forward because of previous abuse. God is calling us to be free in the Spirit.

Scripture: For though we live in the world, we do not wage war as the world does. The weapons we fight with are not the weapons of the world. On the contrary, they have divine power to demolish strongholds. We demolish arguments and every pretension that sets itself up against the knowledge of God, and we take captive every thought to make it obedient to Christ. And we will be ready to punish every act of disobedience, once your obedience is complete. **2 Corinthians 10:3-6**

My Thoughts for Making Lemonade:

_____

_____

_____

_____

_____

_____

_____

_____

_____

_____

_____

BUMPER STICKERS

How often have you been behind a car with a bumper sticker? Some of the bumper stickers boast of "wanting to fish," "having great children at school," or it may display the name of the candidate someone who wants to win an election. Bumper stickers give way to our beliefs and personality. If you follow someone with athletic stickers on their car, he or she probably play or enjoy sports. Daily, we as individuals display a bumper sticker. We display our current mood by the way we dress and speak. Our clothing and conversation becomes a bumper sticker because we convey our views, thoughts, and personality through our dress. So who do men say that you are?

Scripture: Jesus and his disciples went on to the villages around Caesarea Philippi. On the way he asked them, "Who do people say I am?" They replied, "Some say John the Baptist; others say Elijah; and still others, one of the prophets." "But what about you?" he asked. "Who do you say I am?" Peter answered, "You are the Christ. Jesus warned them not to tell anyone about him. **Mark 8:27-30**

 My Thoughts for Making Lemonade:

_____

_____

_____

_____

_____

_____

_____

_____

_____

_____

_____

_____

_____

_____

_____

_____

_____

_____

_____

_____

_____

_____

_____

_____

_____

THE PAST

Why is it so easy for us to want to remember the time when a specific event happened or took place? Why do we dwell on our past successes, failures, and hurts. The word "past" is defined as: history, former, gone, elapsed, or having taken place in a period before. If we cannot bring time back, why do we try to bring back, the past? Our hope is built on the prosperity of Christ, and He does not live in the past. He continues to tell us to "press forward."

Scripture: Brothers, I do not consider myself yet to have taken hold of it. But one thing I do: Forgetting what is behind and straining toward what is ahead I press on toward the goal to win the prize for which God has called me heavenward in Christ Jesus. **Philippians 3:13-14**

My Thoughts for Making Lemonade:

_____

_____

_____

_____

_____

AIR MATTRESS

Life experiences seem a very easy way for God to teach life lessons. Sometimes we use an air mattress when we take extended trips. Often when we are ready to leave and the mattress has to be deflated. We will release the valve but become impatient when the air is draining slowly so we try to force it out. What usually happens then is, it becomes more difficult to release and we become frustrated often having to walk away. Life is the same way when we try to help Christ. We get frustrated when the results are not what we want. Christ wants us to trust Him in every area of our lives.

Scripture: Trust in the lord with all your heart and lean not on your own understanding; in all your ways acknowledge him, and he will make your paths straight. **Proverbs 3:5-6**

My Thoughts for Making Lemonade:

_____

_____

_____

_____

LIFE GUARD

When you are having fun at the pool or beach, the lifeguard is the last person you may think about, but his job is very important. He is responsible for keeping an eye on everybody and the surroundings to ensure the safety of those who are in the waters. He cannot sleep or become distracted because if he does, someone may lose their life. He is trained in life saving procedures and can spot danger afar off. Christ never sleeps nor slumbers. He is committed to saving our life.

Scripture: You will keep in perfect peace him whose mind is steadfast, because he trusts in you. Trust in the lord forever, for the lord, the lord, is the Rock eternal.

Isaiah 26:3-24

My Thoughts for Making Lemonade:

_____

_____

_____

_____

_____

RAINBOWS

Rainbows can be seen big, bright, and beautiful after a heavy rain or storm. During that time the individual may have had to take cover because the storm may have been catastrophic. However, after all of the showers, the grass appears greener and fresher, and everyone is happier because of the bow in the sky as we remember the promise. The promise being, that the earth will never be destroyed by water again. When we're in a personal storm it is difficult to remember that we will not die in our current circumstances even though they are challenging for the moment. Some of the best rainbows are after the worst storms, but our light afflictions are but for a season.

Scripture: We are hard pressed on every side, but not crushed; perplexed, but not in despair; persecuted, but not abandoned; struck down, but not destroyed. We always carry around in our body the death of Jesus, so that the life of Jesus may also be revealed in our body.

2 Corinthians 4:8-10

My Thoughts for Making Lemonade:

WHAT WOULD YOU DO?

You have heard commercials on television talk about what you would do for an item. We have had friends and family to ask us: "what would you do if..." Often they are asking for permission, asking for information, or our opinion. Depending on the circumstances that question would require a lot of thought. Think of the strong desire the individual needs to have just to follow through on the answer to the question. Have you ever considered what you would do for your salvation? What will you do for Christ? What will you do to inherit eternal life? How important is it to you? Will you give your life to Christ?

Scripture: What good is it for a man to gain the whole world, yet forfeit his soul? Or what can a man give in exchange for his soul? **Mark 8:36-37**

My Thoughts for Making Lemonade:

_____

_____

_____

_____

_____

BRANDS AND SYMBOLS

Everything is known by a name. It may be the name established from the foundation of the earth or a name that was assigned to a newly designed or discovered item. We are able to recognize businesses or cars by the brand or symbol they display. Universally we know that hospitals have ambulances, and firemen have red fire trucks, and police-officers have blue uniforms. They all have sirens that identify who they are when they're engaged in an emergency. If it's so easy to identify these things or people around us by the symbol or brands then why do we have a difficult time identifying the saints?

Scripture: When Jesus came to the region of Caesarea Philippi, he asked his disciples, "Who do people say the Son of Man is?" They replied, "Some say John the Baptist, others say Elijah; and still others, Jeremiah or one of the prophets. "But what about you?" he asked. "Who do you say I am?" Simon Peter answered, "You are the Christ, the Son of the living God." Jesus replied, "Blessed are you, Simon son of Jonah, for this was not revealed to you by man, but by my Father in heaven. And I tell you that you are Peter, and on this rock I will build my church, and the gates of Hades will not overcome it. **Matthew 16:13-18**

My Thoughts for Making Lemonade:

_____

_____

_____

_____

_____

_____

_____

_____

_____

_____

_____

_____

_____

_____

_____

_____

_____

_____

TATS

A tattoo sometimes referred to as body modification or body art is a permanent change in the integrity of the skin and is a matter of choice for some and forced on others as a form of identification. This is considered branding. Joseph Banks, a naturalist, stated in 1769 that tattoos mark the person's humor or disposition. This includes status or rank, spiritual devotion, decorations for bravery, sexual lures, punishment, protection, and pledges of love. Some tattoos are placed cosmetically or medically as with some celebrities with whom we may be familiar. A few Christian groups wear tattoos to show allegiance; therefore, they take a more liberal or neutral position, while other religions such as Mormonism, Islam, and Judaism see it as pagan, believing it should be forbidden according to Leviticus 19:28 which says, "Ye shall not make any cuttings in your flesh for the dead, nor print any marks upon you: I am the Lord." (From www.biblegateway.com – King James Version)

Scripture: One man considers one day more sacred than another; another man considers every day alike. Each one should be fully convinced in his own mind. He, who regards one day as special, does so to the Lord. He, who eats meat, eats to the Lord, for he gives thanks to God; and he who abstains, does so to the Lord and gives thanks to God. For none of us lives to himself alone and none of us die to himself alone. If we live, we live to the Lord; and if we die, we die to the Lord. So, whether we live or die, we belong to the Lord. For this very reason, Christ died and returned to life so that he might be the Lord of both the dead and the living. You, then, why do you judge your brother? Or why do you look down on your brother? For we will all stand before God's judgment seat. It is written: "As surely as I live, says the Lord, every knee will bow before me;" **Romans 14:5-11**

My Thoughts for Making Lemonade:

_____

_____

_____

_____

_____

_____

_____

_____

THE SUPER CENTER

If you pay close attention, you will notice many people attending the community church, called the "Super Center." I have often wondered why people would attend this center twenty-four hours a day. They come in as families, individuals, women, men, gays, lesbians, and all races and ethnic backgrounds because it's a universal center. Everyone is accepted! While in the Super Center the guest move aimlessly from one aisle to another sometimes in a thoughtless fashion and some with purpose. Some attend just to see if there is anything different than what they saw just twenty-fours earlier. Many come and leave without purchasing anything at all, or some come and make purchases that will sustain them for a period of time. Spiritually, we do the same thing when we attend church on a weekly basis; some people come aimlessly down the aisle and not receive anything while others receive what they need to sustain them over a period of time: however, if we keep coming we will eventually get something, and it will be exactly what we need.

Scripture: I rejoiced with those who said to me, "Let us go to the house of the Lord." Our feet are standing in your gates, O Jerusalem. Jerusalem is built like a city that is closely compacted together. That is where the tribes go up, the tribes of the Lord, to praise the name of the Lord according to the statute given to Israel. **Psalms 122:1-4**

My Thoughts for Making Lemonade:

_____

_____

_____

_____

_____

_____

_____

_____

_____

_____

_____

_____

_____

_____

_____

_____

_____

TREES

Trees are identified by their seed, branches and trunk. Trees have the ability to reproduce and in it lay the DNA of the new tree. As the children of God, we have everything in us to reproduce ourselves. Whatever gift or call we have on your life is already in us. God placed the DNA in us from the foundation of the earth. The only reason a tree will not produce is because it's dead. The stump of a tree will produce if it has not been removed from the earth. God needs us to produce what he has placed in us. Be fruitful and multiply. The tree is never for itself, but it offers shade, food, or shelter for those that may come.

Scripture: May God Almighty bless you and make you fruitful. **Genesis 28:3**

My Thoughts for Making Lemonade:

_____

_____

_____

_____

_____

BATTER UP

When a baseball player wants to increase his batting statistics, he often attends what we call "batting practice." The balls are released to the batter by a disengaged machine at a rate previously and precisely set for the current batter. The batter is able to increase his confidence the more he makes contact with the balls. He is able to judge distance and timing so that he can adjust his swing. He knows the rules of the game; therefore, he is only honing his skills. Within the game of life, we know the rules. The test comes so that we can increase our faith and to make better contact with the Lord when we pray. Sometimes the batter has to change his bat to make better contact. The current bat may not have the necessary weight needed to make the contact. As with our faith, sometimes it has to be adjusted based on the test.

Scripture: For we walk by faith, not by sight.
2 Corinthians 5:7

 My Thoughts for Making Lemonade:

SELF-CHECK

Each month young girls and women are encouraged to do a self-breast check. What many may not know is that men get breast cancers also, and should check their breasts as well. Women are encouraged to call a sister or friend and encourage her to do the monthly exam; therefore, that friend is accountable to someone. If we're able to respond when someone encourages us to maintain our health, why are we offended when our brother or sister in the Lord corrects us to keep us spiritually healthy?

Scripture: Examine yourselves to see whether you are in the faith; test yourselves. Do you not realize that Christ Jesus is in you —unless, of course, you fail the test? And I trust that you will discover that we have not failed the test. Now we pray to God that you will not do anything wrong. Not that people will see that we have stood the test but that you will do what is right even though we may seem to have failed. For we cannot do anything against the truth, but only for the truth. **2 Corinthians 13:5-8**

 My Thoughts for Making Lemonade:

DRIVE-UP

Most fast food establishments usually have pictures of what you can order from the drive-up window. What you see and what you get may be two totally different things because of the method of preparation. Most often we are not familiar with the preparation process for the menu items; we just know that it doesn't take long to prepare them. Often when Christ has called us to do something, it may not be known what we are to do nor do we understand the process of how we are shaped and molded. We may desire what someone else has; not realizing that each is a special order and was created especially for a work. Therefore, don't desire what another man has.

Scripture: For I know the plans I have for you," declares the Lord, "plans to prosper you and not to harm you, plans to give you hope and a future. **Jeremiah 29:11**

My Thoughts for Making Lemonade:

_____

_____

_____

LOST BALLS

How often do we lose our focus, our confidence, or our drive and never make a decision to go back and reposition ourselves. We count it as lost. I was watching batting practice one day for a local baseball team when three balls came over the fence. After about an hour, the "lost treasures" were retrieved by someone from the practice field. The balls have value to a baseball player, but little worth to anyone else. We refuse to inconvenience ourselves to retrieve what is rightly ours-our relationship with Christ.

Scripture: Suppose a woman has ten silver coins and loses one. Does she not light a lamp, sweep the house and search carefully until she finds it? And when she finds it, she calls her friends and neighbors together and says, "Rejoice with me; I have found my lost coin." In the same way, I tell you, there is rejoicing in the presence of the angels of God over one sinner who repents. **Luke 15:8-10**

My Thoughts for Making Lemonade:

_____

_____

_____

_____

_____

_____

_____

_____

_____

_____

_____

_____

_____

_____

_____

_____

_____

_____

_____

_____

_____

_____

_____

_____

DAVID

You have had friends who could attract any guy or girl they wanted, but they wanted to talk to the individual who was already in a relationship. It does not matter to them that the person is in a relationship because it's what they want at the time. David was the same way. He could have had anyone, but he chose Uriah's wife, got her pregnant and had her husband killed so that he could have her; he impregnated her and the baby later died (II Samuel 11:1-5, II Samuel 12:14). We need to think when we begin to desire something or someone that is not ours. There are grave consequences for our actions, and lives may be changed forever.

Scripture: Have mercy on me, O God, according to your unfailing love; according to your great compassion blot out my transgressions. Wash away all my iniquity and cleanse me from my sin. For I know my transgressions, and my sin is always before me. Against you, you only, have I sinned and done what is evil in your sight, so that you are proved right when you speak and justified when you judge. Surely I was sinful at birth, sinful from the time my mother conceived me. Surely you desire truth in the inner parts; you teach me wisdom in the inmost place. Cleanse me with hyssop, and I will be clean; wash me, and I will be whiter than snow. Let me hear joy and gladness; let the bones you have crushed rejoice. Hide your face from my sins and blot out all my iniquity. Create in me a pure heart, O God, and renew a steadfast spirit within me. Do not cast me from your presence or take your Holy Spirit from me. Restore to me the joy of your salvation and grant me a willing spirit, to sustain me. Then I will teach transgressors your ways, and sinners will turn back to you. Save me from bloodguilt, O God, the God who saves me, and my tongue will sing of your righteousness. O Lord, open my lips, and my mouth will declare your praise. You do not delight in sacrifice, or I would bring it; you do not take pleasure in burnt offerings. The sacrifices of God are a broken spirit; a broken and contrite heart, O God, you will not despise.

Psalm 51:1-17

My Thoughts for Making Lemonade:

_____

_____

_____

_____

FAITH

Do you see yourself doing the impossible? Have you ever tried to do what you think you can't do? Would you say it is better to try and fail than to not try at all? What would happen if you tried and succeeded? Would you have more confidence? So are you saying that faith is no more than confidence you have in the ability that Christ has given you, to be able to accomplish something for Him? Christ has given us a unique ability to accomplish great things. Search yourself, whatever you find yourself always doing is probably your gift. So stir up your gift.

Scripture: Now faith is being sure of what we hope for and certain of what we do not see. **Hebrews 11:1**

My Thoughts for Making Lemonade:

_____

_____

_____

_____

_____

ONE MARY

The young girl who has her entire life ahead of her is engaged to be married, but before she could get married she got pregnant for another. Can you imagine the conversation in the neighborhood? She wasn't trying to get pregnant. It just happened. She did not attempt to trap the man because she was a virgin. She was saving herself for marriage. Sometimes the man has a greater understanding of worldly things so we have to make sure we are engaged to the right man. Don't be married to the wrong man when the right one comes. You are chosen to do something great; Mary was the mother of Jesus.

Scripture: In the sixth month, God sent the angel Gabriel to Nazareth, a town in Galilee, to a virgin pledged to be married to a man named Joseph, a descendant of David. The virgin's name was Mary. The angel went to her and said, "Greetings, you who are highly favored! The Lord is with you." Mary was greatly troubled at his words and wondered what kind of greeting this might be. But the angel said to her, "Do not be afraid, Mary, you have found favor with God. You will be with child and give birth to a son, and you are to give him the name Jesus, He will be great and will be called the Son of the Most High.

Luke 1:26-31a

My Thoughts for Making Lemonade:

_____

_____

_____

_____

_____

_____

_____

_____

_____

_____

_____

_____

_____

_____

_____

_____

ROSES

The euphoria, includes the smell, the color, the size, and texture which all determines a magnificent rose. Roses represent love, beauty, compassion and sincerity. But did you ever stop to think of the Gardner who had to harvest the rose and how painful it may have been for him to gather the lovely flowers for your delight, but we appreciate the beauty. We forget the pain that Christ had to suffer to give us eternal life. We only look for the day of His return; we forget that when we place the rose in the beautiful vase it still has thorns; therefore, if we're going to enjoy the beauty of salvation, we need to understand that there maybe some thorns.

Scripture: The thief comes only to steal and kill and destroy; I have come that they may have life, and have it to the full. **John 10:10**

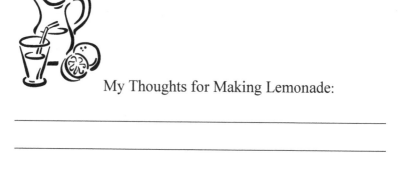 My Thoughts for Making Lemonade:

_____

_____

_____

HOW TO MAKE LEMONADE

We have heard it said more than once, "when life gives you lemons make lemonade," the problem is no one ever tells you how to make the lemonade. No one takes the time to tell you that sometimes life comes bitter to everyone; but it is your choice how you chose to respond. A lemon is a bitter fruit, but if sugar is added, it becomes a refreshing drink. When frozen lemonade is made, the entire fruit is pulverized, with heat added; to capture the full essence of the favor. If heat is being increased in your life, there is something else in you the Lord is attempting to bring to the surface. So when life sends you a bitter situation ask yourself, what positive lesson can I learn from this situation or is there something in this for someone else? Decide how you can glorify God in your life through the trials and opposition that come your way. Look for strong spiritual leadership and follow the great teaching. One thing for sure, the Lord will not put more on you than you can bear. If we refuse the lemons in our life because of the bitter flavor, we will miss the greater treat. One lemon will only provide three tablespoons of juice; therefore, you need several lemons to make great lemonade! The trials and battles in our life are the opportunities to collect lemons.

The more lemons we collect the more lemonade we are able to make and serve. We serve others out of our abundant supply. Therefore, the lemons you are collecting maybe to refresh someone else. Remember when sweet is added to bitter it becomes refreshing! Once we have learned to conquer the trials in our life He will bring us to a place of peace.

Scripture: No temptation has seized you except what is common to man. And God is faithful; he will not let you be tempted beyond what you can bear. But when you are tempted, he will also provide a way out so that you can stand up under it. **I Corinthians 10:13**

Do not be anxious about anything, but in everything, by prayer and petition, with thanksgiving, present your requests to God, and the peace of God, which transcends all understanding, will guard your hearts and your minds in Christ Jesus. **Philippians 4:6-7**

My Thoughts for Making Lemonade:

_____

_____

About the Author

Melanie Dees is a powerful woman of God that desires to encourage and transform the minds and hearts of those around her. She is an Associate Pastor in ministry at Grace Cathedral Christian Fellowship Ministries, Sumter South Carolina. Her rural upbringing in Micanopy, Florida, military travels, and years in ministry has given her a keen insight into people; which she uses to bring the Word and Work of God to a place of easy understanding. She believes that Ministry is far beyond the walls of the church building and we are all ministers of the Gospel. Melanie Dees can be contacted by emailing her at the following email address: deeshowtomakelemonade@yahoo.com

References

Scriptural references are from Pardis Version 5:1, Zondervan
Interactive Bible – Copyright 2002-2004

What is a Diamond?
Contributed by: Gemological Institute of America "Gemstones,"
Microsoft® Encarta® Online Encyclopedia 2005
http://encarta.msn.com © 1997-2005 Microsoft Corporation. All
Rights Reserved. © 1993-2005 Microsoft Corporation. All
Rights Reserved.
http://encarta.msn.com/encyclopedia_761563821/Gemstones.html